Schools:
How Parents Can Make a Difference

Schools:
How Parents Can Make a Difference

by
ETHEL HERR

MOODY PRESS
CHICAGO

Unless otherwise noted, all Scripture quotations are from the King James Version.

The use of selected references from various versions of the Bible in this publication does not necessarily imply publisher endorsement of the versions in their entirety.

Library of Congress Cataloging in Publication Data

Herr, Ethel L.
   Schools, how parents can make a difference.
   Includes bibliographical references.
   1. Home and school—United States. 2. Christian education of children—United States. I. Title.

LC225.3.H47   649'.68   81-11034

ISBN 0-8024-1163-O   AACR2

CONTENTS

CHAPTER   **PAGE**

	Dedication	6
	Foreword	7
	Acknowledgments	8
	Introduction—A Word of Hope	11
1.	Who Is the Culprit?	15
2.	Setting Our Goals	23
3.	Playing Our Roles	31
4.	Getting Ready for School	39
5.	What Are the Alternatives?	51
6.	Choosing the Best School	61
7.	Cooperating, Supplementing, Trusting	71
8.	What Are Our Rights?	81
9.	Getting Action	91
10.	Who Pays the Bills and How?	101
11.	The Textbook Arena	111
12.	Volunteers Are VIPs	121
13.	Paid and Appointed Involvement	129
14.	Our Needs Are Special	137
15.	Our Needs Are Special, Too	147
16.	Arming for the Future	157
17.	Resource List	163
	Glossary	178
	Appendix 1—Parish Support for Public Schools	184
	Appendix 2—How to Have an Effective Parent/Teacher Conference	186
	Appendix 3—The Television Generation	188
	Appendix 4—Key Communicators	199
	Appendix 5—How to Start a Parent Organization	204
	Appendix 6—How to Write a Letter for Action	206
	Appendix 7—Nineteen Suggestions for Checking Rising Cost of Education Without Cutting Quality	207
	Appendix 8—"Would a State Voucher System Work?"	209
	Appendix 9—Transcendental Meditation Is a Variation of the Heathen Hinduism	212
	Appendix 10—Sample Letter Requesting Sex Education Information	216

For Trish
Creative spark
Warm-fuzzy confidant
Educator *par excellence*
True friend.
Thank you, Tricia Bubenik.

NOTE

Throughout this book I have used the pronoun *he* when referring to students, parents, and administrators. References to teachers and aides are indicated by the pronoun *she*.

FOREWORD

Ethel Herr hits the nail right on the head when she advocates that parents are the hope for their child's education by being co-partners with the school in advancing the learning process. Parents must be involved in their children's education, for statistics show us there is no doubt that they make a significant difference in their children's academic growth. This is a practical, straightforward, hard-hitting book. As a parent I welcome this book to my home. As an educator I applaud the fact that a parent has stood up and said, "We must help the schools, and here are some ways we can do it in a positive, aggressive manner."

Parents do develop a young child's attitude and motivation toward learning before he enters school. We know that language development, a basis for learning, begins at home with parents. The motivation and reinforcement for language proficiency comes directly from the parents. Many of the basic concepts children learn about the world around them come from exposure the parent provides. Parents also model attitudes and the importance of education and learning by their actions. The parent who reads rather than watches television each night models the importance and joy of reading.

It is a natural sequence, therefore, that parents be involved in the schools as a way of continuing input into their child's educational experience. We know from research that parent involvement in a child's learning has a positive effect. A parent shows an interest in the child's world as well as provides motivation for learning.

Learning is a total act; it is more than knowing reading, writing, and arithmetic. A parent who is aware of the content the child is learning in school can reinforce and extend that learning.

Most important, the parent is the child's first teacher as well as the lifelong teacher. Are you flunking out as a teacher-parent?

If you educate a child, you educate a nation. As a Christian I thank God for this book. Ethel Herr has challenged us to a high calling. We must do our part as parents. God asks us to do no less.

ORLEY R. HERRON
President
National College of Education

7

ACKNOWLEDGMENTS

So MANY PEOPLE have edified my life and taught me what I know about education that it would be impossible to mention everyone to whom acknowledgment is due. I could begin with my own mother, who is a talented teacher, serving at home, in the church, and on the mission field. I could include all my school teachers, Sunday school teachers, youth leaders, college professors—on and on the list would go. Many names I have forgotten; I am not even sure who taught me what or when or how. Only here and there names or faces stand out as I associate them with some key lessons I learned. To each one who helped me to believe that the learning/growing process is the most exciting part of life, I want to express a hearty thank-you.

As a mother, volunteer, and guardian of my own children's education, I am especially indebted to the professional educators who encouraged me to be involved, gave me opportunities, and taught me how to use them. Most of all in that category, I am grateful to Tricia Bubenik, expert educator of my children and close personal friend, who worked with me, inspired me, and taught me more than any other person I know. I acknowledge further the administrators, teachers, and school site council members of Sunnyvale (California) Elementary and Fremont Union High School districts for their excellent training in productive involvement for action. I can never forget my gratitude to my children for their patience with me in the learning process and for making parent involvement experiences a pleasant inevitability. To my husband I offer deepest thanks for his support and counsel as he so aptly held up his side of the involvement team.

When I began to research this book my list of supporters burgeoned in my file drawers. Teachers, administrators, friends, friends of friends, organizations, and Christian education leaders from all across the country responded to my questionnaires and personal requests more than generously. I was particularly grateful to the leaders of the Basic Education Leadership Conference and the National Educators Fellowship for allowing me to attend their conventions and interview them. Editors Les Stobbe of *Christian Herald* Book Club and Beverly Burch of Moody Press offered me unlimited enthusiasm and valuable guidance.

As I put it all on paper, my faithful critique group: Andrea, Charlene, Dorothy, Nina, Alice, and Marjorie advised and encouraged me, always prodding me to hurry and finish the book "so we can give it to our friends who need it." As I finished the manuscript my professional friends, Vivien Efting, Rich and Janet Cox, Nancy Pearson, Tricia Bubenik, Grace Hammar, and Nancy Stake read it and shared their suggestions.

Finally, my mother, Alice Funkhouser (first and last on my list), proofread the last draft for all the technical problems she handles with such expertise.

Such fathers as commit their sons to tutors and teachers and themselves never witness or overhear their instructions deserve rebuke, for they fall far short of their obligation. They ought themselves to undertake examination of their children and not place their trust in the disposition of a wage earner; even the latter will bestow greater care on the children if they know that they will periodically be called to account. [Plutarch, 120 A.D.]

INTRODUCTION

A WORD OF HOPE

WHEN YOU READ the newspaper headlines do you sometimes wonder whether there is hope for modern education? Do reports of campus violence and lack of discipline, sexual permissiveness and drunkenness among teens, declining test scores, and teacher strikes make you question whether it ever will be safe to entrust the minds and characters of our children to the schools of our communities? Did you ever ask what, if anything, we can do to make education work for the next generation?

Parents, grandparents, and other concerned citizens all over America are asking those same questions today. Consider two young mothers visiting at a Sunday school picnic.

"Our daughter is starting school this fall," said the first woman. "It's rather scary. Should we go to the expense of a Christian day school or is the public school safe enough? How can we know what is best for her?"

"We're facing the same problem," said the second woman. "If only there were a book of some kind that would help us decide what to do!"

About the time the first of our three children graduated from high school, the idea for such a book was born in my mind. For thirteen years we had trained our children, attended school functions, made friends with teachers, worked on volunteer projects, served on committees, and made our views known to educators of all ranks. We had struggled with the wide variety of problems common to all modern parents in the process of trying to secure a quality education for our children. Often confused, we had had to pray and work our way through the problems—sometimes finding solutions, often blundering, but always learning. *Perhaps*, I thought, *I can share some of this learning with a new generation of parents.*

11

I began digging through libraries, writing letters, collecting questionnaires, subscribing to newsletters, interviewing educators, and attending conferences. In the process my mood fluctuated between the heights of visionary enthusiasm and the lowlands of despair. Along with some fascinating and helpful insights and suggestions, my research turned up a distressing number of negative attitudes and frightening facts.

Then one day when I was stuffed to my limit with facts and theories, wrestling to sort out my reactions and decide whether I could write the book and remain both honest and positive, a friend asked, "What are you writing these days?"

I had hardly mentioned my topic when she interrupted, reciting for me some shocking things she had heard about the hopeless state of education and its unbelievably bleak future.

My response was a quick defense. "But there are still things that parents can do if they just know how and go to work. Besides, some good things are happening in education today."

Unconvinced, my friend challenged me, "If you can find anything positive to offer, I promise I'll read it!"

Something in her skeptical tone revived my own uneasiness. "Dear Lord," I prayed as I headed down the freeway toward home that day, "is it possible that after spending all this time in research I must admit that I have been unrealistic? Times are getting worse. Maybe it is hopeless and I should scrap the whole project before I get in any deeper."

No sooner had I voiced the words than my confusion began to melt away. Looking back over my years of being the mother of Martha, Tim, and Mary, I detected an answer emerging. During the years my husband and I had worked in many capacities as VIPs (Voluntarily Involved Parents), we had wondered why so few parents seemed to share our active concern. Somehow we felt certain that an enormous amount of potential for solving the problems of modern education lay with the parents whose children were our children's classmates.

Now I thought I understood why. Too many of the powerful people—parents, educators, and church leaders—had been deceived by the clever logic of an old satanic lie. It was the same lie that had nagged at me periodically through my months of research. It went something like this:

Why try now? The situation is beyond help. The best you can do is to look around for someone else to blame. Gripe all you want to neighbors or newspaper editors, but whatever you do, do not try anything constructive. You do not know enough to work effectively. Besides, this is the beginning of the inevitable end!

The moment I recognized the subtlety of the lie, I knew that I was not only free to write this book—I *must* do it. With beautiful clarity I saw the simple key to the dilemma. Other generations of parents before us have faced severe educational and moral crises. Like them, we too must go on parenting, no matter how bad our circumstances.

This only becomes possible when we consider the nature of the God we serve, the God who entrusted our children into our keeping in the first place. He has never forsaken even the least of His children in their need and confusion. He is not about to begin forsaking us now.

Instead, He has followed us into the tight, little corners we have fashioned through our ignorance, lack of experience, fear, and neglect. If we are willing to give up brooding about the gloom and working ourselves into a frenzy as we try to decide where to shift the blame, He stands ready to show us a positive way out of our negative position.

As I sit down to write this book, I am excited to pass on to you some of the fascinating, practical advice that the Lord has brought to my husband and me over our years of success, failure, and research. I have sifted through stacks of accumulated materials to glean those ideas that I trust can help you the most.

I do not know what your ideas are about education. You may believe in the value of public education and object to private or Christian schools. You may be committed to the private or Christian school approach, having despaired of the public school at least for your children's generation. Perhaps you are perplexed by the whole situation and not sure how to make up your mind. Regardless of your personal philosophy or commitment, this book addresses itself to your needs.

If you are looking for a book with easy, pat answers and cure-all solutions—the do-this-and-all-your-problems-will-vanish kind—then you are reading between the wrong two covers. I do not have all the answers. Those I have uncovered are usually complex, because the subject is complex.

If you are looking for some guidelines, facts, insights, and challenges to assist you in thinking and praying through your situation to make the God-directed choices necessary for your child's education, I trust that you will not be disappointed here.

The subject of parent involvement in education is overwhelming. I have made no attempt to present any exhaustive treatment of it; that would take a multivolume encyclopedia. Instead, I have tried to help you to see that you, the parents, can do something to make education work for your children.

When choosing between the many ideas that have crossed my life and my desk, I have screened them for four characteristics:

(1) Is it *inspirational?* Will it challenge and entice you, the reader, to try something similar?

(2) Is it *positive?* Even if some of the actions we must take will be negative, their end thrust must be positive. One parent put it this way: "You can never have power unless you are positive."

(3) Is it *specific?* I know from experience how difficult it is to translate generalities into action. In many cases I will refer you to other sources of detailed information on a given topic.

(4) Is it *practical?* Has it worked for me or someone else? If not, then I will not bother to tell you about it. This book is not built on untried theories, but on workable solutions to real problems.

Above all, to the two young mothers, my skeptical friends, and to all the perplexed parents who read these pages, I want to offer a strong positive word of hope. Until God abdicates His throne to man and Christian parents abdicate their responsibilities to some "system," education will never be a hopeless cause or an irreversible downhill plunge to disaster.

1

WHO IS THE CULPRIT?

The more complicated the society, the more difficult the path to education.[1]

Francesco Cordasco

AT THE HEART of every community in America stands an aging castle atop a gray, craggy hill. Over the entryway of the multistoried structure, one word is ornately carved in marble: EDUCATION.

Our grandparents built this hallowed institution. Our parents lived in unquestioning awe of it. But our generation?

We form siege lines around it. Dazzling banners wave from every corner of a growing encampment below the ivy-smothered stone ramparts. Behind the lines, concerned citizens are busy forging pruning-hooks into spears, preparing for battle. Parents and news teams, businessmen and lawmakers, churches and patriotic organizations are all eyeing the fortresses of education—both public and private, Christian and non-Christian—with increasing suspicion.

At the foot of the hill, sharp recruiting officers from a dozen different regiments canvass the neighborhoods where we live. Armed with emotionally charged accounts of classroom atrocities, each pressures us to enlist in his unit *now*—while there is time.

Many of us are confused about the true nature of the problem. We fear to join what may prove to be either a needless cause or a doomed one. We are even more fearful of staging a fanatical confrontation with our impressionable children trapped in between.

To enlist or not to enlist—we are led to believe that this is the decision we face. In actuality that decision was made for us centuries ago, when God through Solomon said: "Train up a child in the way he should go" (Proverbs 22:6). Parenthood involves an automatic enlistment in the army dedicated to protecting the minds and characters of our children and to helping them grow into mature adults.

The real decision every parent faces today is not whether to fight but how. And what? On which battlefield? With which regiment? Using which weapons?

This book was written to guide you as you (1) identify the enemy, or source, of your educational problems, (2) evaluate your situation, identifying both the good and bad elements, (3) find your battlefield, and (4) plan your strategy.

Perhaps you have found as I did, that many of the most crucial battles must be fought quite peaceably. Actually, I have often felt much more like a helper or a nurse than a soldier. Although I have encountered problems that do demand radical solutions and loud protestations, what amazes me is the large number of difficulties that dissolve in the warmth of a positive helping hand.

Having said all this, we must never forget that we are indeed in a battle. Regardless of our weapons—peaceful or militant—we are basically at war. Because of that, we need to maintain a vigilant attitude in our efforts to provide safe and high quality education for our children. But we want to avoid one well-set trap that snares many sincere parents. Aroused to panic by some serious situation, we may rush into battle, start swinging a sword, and cut off all the wrong heads. In the end we will do irreparable harm and effectively hinder the parental involvement process. Before we choose a battlefield and join a regiment, we must first take time to ask: What or whom are we fighting, anyway?

If that question confuses you, do not think you are alone. In fact, the word that best describes the growing battle is *confusion*. Everybody is swinging a sword. Each regiment of the army has chosen a different target as the "culprit." Often they fight one another. Even those who work in the "education castle" engage in frequent combat behind the stone walls.

The only thing that all seem to agree upon is the idea that "our educational system is in bad condition."[2] However, everybody has his own idea of who and/or what is to blame. Depending upon which expert you listen to, you may be convinced that any one of the following is the real enemy. In the process of my involvement and research, I have encountered all of these views:

1. *The public school system:* Cold, impersonal, machinelike, it

rules the lives of our children and controls our communities by means of an unreasonable escalation of tax monies.

2. *Teachers:* No good ones are left. All they care about are their own pocketbooks, their right to strike, and their three-month European tours.

3. *National teacher organizations:* With powerful lobbying influence and ability to inspire teachers to demand selfish rights, they are dangerous.

4. *Governmental controls:* Parents contend that education run by the bureaucracy cannot be sensitive to the needs of our children. Administrators moan under the increasing load of unrealistic government regulations and paperwork.

5. *Textbooks:* Often produced at taxpayers' expense, composed of experimental programs and filled with anti-Christian values, they are creating a new generation that is incapable of responsible leadership or respectable citizenship.

6. *Parents:* Many refuse to care for and discipline their children and prohibit educators from doing so.

7. *Unrealistic demands of society:* Citizens are asking schools to do too many things in addition to teaching the three Rs.

8. *Taxpayers:* Revolting by way of citizen ballot initiatives, they cut off the lifeblood of the school system. Yet they still expect peak performance returns on their grudgingly meager investments.

9. *Administrators:* Power-hungry and out of touch with students and parents, they are more interested in political advancement than in Johnny's reading ability.

10. *Rapid changes in modern society:* These are described by one educator in this way: ". . . the world in which we live, where children of five have already incorporated into their everyday thinking ideas that most of the elders will never fully assimilate. Within the lifetime of ten-year-olds the world has entered a new age."[3]

11. *Communism:* Degeneration of education is part of the communist plot to overthrow the government peacefully and imperceptibly.

12. *Atheistic psychologists and educators:* They have sold the public system a ghastly assortment of programs designed to destroy our nation's Judeo-Christian moral value system and replace it with man-centered relativistic humanism.

Each of those accusations probably contains at least a small element of truth. No doubt, we can find examples of each one—some more than others. If today's education fails, all of those factors may have to share in the blame. But none of them is the real enemy. Instead, they are some of the tactical tools being used against us by some strong master-minded enemy.

Who then is this *enemy?* I wrestled long with that question. We might call the enemy ignorance, but ignorance is a condition, not a person with power to plan strategies and employ tactical tools. When I first began to suspect the answer, I set it aside, afraid it was too simplistic. But the further I searched, the more convinced I became that ultimately, behind all our problems, lies the same enemy that we fight in every other area of personal life and society—our age-old enemy, Satan himself. I came to the conclusion that when the apostle Paul wrote, "For we wrestle not against flesh and blood, but against principalities, against powers, against the rulers of the darkness of this world, against spiritual wickedness in high places," (Ephesians 6:12), he was referring to Satan's intrusion even into the education of our children.

In education as in other fields of human experience, this ultimate source and personification of evil poses quite respectably as the spirit of human self-sufficiency. He convinces the unwary that we can solve our own problems, determine our own destiny, and bring about our own utopia—all of this without help from or reference to an absolute God. Even Christians become subtly drawn into his way of thinking if we are not careful.

An essential first step is to identify our enemy, but when we try to plan our battle strategy, we can become both confused and discouraged as we listen to all the recruiting officers in the Battle for Quality Education. Each one has a plausible line to support his approach. Furthermore, he has a specific solution proposal, a guaranteed-to-work battle tactic, complete with a rigidly prescribed arsenal of weapons. The problem is that his battle strategy and weapons are effective in dealing, not with the enemy, but only with one or more of that enemy's tactics.

We do need to fight the satanic tactics. In fact, the rest of this book deals with methods for doing just that. Yet we must never fool ourselves into thinking that to frustrate one tactic signals the end of the battle. To move a child into a Christian school, for example, may solve many problems, but it will not stop Satan from making our battle both necessary and difficult.

We need to avoid the common error of thinking that when a child fails in school (either academically, socially, or morally), it must be the school's fault. The primary responsibility for a child's education lies with his parents, not with any kind of school system—public, private, or Christian. Charles R. Swindoll, in his book *You and Your Child*, observes: "I have come to realize that neither the church nor the school can resurrect what the home puts to death."[4]

Far more educational problems originate in our homes than we realize. The few that actually do begin in the school can usually be solved by alert and sensitive parents in the home.

A friend of mine shared with me the story of how the Lord taught her this important lesson. By all standards her first child was the perfect baby. Good-natured, pleasant, intelligent, cooperative—what more could a parent ask? When she started school her progress confirmed her parents' belief that their child was special indeed.

Then came their son. From day one he proved to be totally different. Extremely active, he operated a perpetual mischief-making business. When he started kindergarten, the papers he brought home shrieked of impending disaster. Before the school term was half over, the boy's teacher called the mother in for a conference.

"Your son is simply too immature for school," she said. "If things don't improve by June, I think you should seriously consider having him repeat kindergarten."

The parents were shocked. To them, as to most young and inexperienced parents, holding a child back in school seemed a near tragedy. They prayed and hoped for a change that would make such drastic measures unnecessary, but the boy's daily papers showed no evidence of the anticipated improvement.

Though no one suggested running tests to see if he had some special learning problem, the mother today believes he was simply slow in developing motor coordination skills.

"I know now that comparing our children wasn't good," my friend says. "But I simply couldn't help it. Our daughter was so perfect, and my little guy was such a pill. His schoolwork was awful! I couldn't understand why he had to be so different."

After much prayer the anxious parents took the teacher's advice and enrolled their son once more in kindergarten—this time in a Christian school. Surely if anyone could give him the extra help he obviously needed, those dedicated teachers could.

But the papers coming home were still dreadful. Once more, in

November, the mother was called to a teacher conference. "This is not a school problem," the teacher suggested. "It is a home problem. If he is to change and begin to learn, it is up to you."

"*Me?*" my friend gasped. "But I'm no educator. Whatever could I do?"

"Yes, *you*," the teacher repeated. "Your son has absolutely no self-confidence. You must begin to praise his work."

"How can I do that? Everything he does is terrible!"

"Every day when he comes home from school, take time to sit down and look at each paper," was the simple answer. "No matter how messy it is, you can find something good in it to praise."

The days that followed were a great challenge as the mother began learning how to stop comparing children and to minor on mistakes while majoring on positive reactions.

"That was a huge turning point in my relationship with my young son," she remembers. "He didn't change overnight, but I did. Then he responded, changing slowly. By the time he was eight years old, he was a different boy, bringing home papers to be proud of."

Repeatedly, that mother thanks the Lord that He showed her the true nature of the enemy's tactics before it was too late to correct her strategy and rescue a life.

Knowing that Satan is the ultimate enemy we fight frees us to approach each problem with a total-picture perspective. Then we can learn to handle the difficulties of recognizing our own personal responsibility and relating to other parents and educators. All who know anything about Satan know that his most effective technique has been to pop up wherever and whenever we least expect him. Our Bibles assure us that he is a loser with a predictably gloomy future. As someone has said, "Roar he or purr, he is a defeated foe." Knowing all this, with confidence and divine optimism we can begin to "resist the devil and he will flee from [us]" (James 4:7).

It also helps to realize that this battle is a cooperative effort. No one family can tackle the enemy on every front. That does not give us license to sit down and do nothing, simply because we cannot do everything. Instead, we are each responsible to prayerfully select the specific areas of battle where we will be involved.

One of the first places to look for guidance in choosing our battlefield is in the area of priorities. We all know that next to our marriages, our children are the most important responsibility God has given to us. That is why we are ready to act in the first place. But in our eagerness to translate theory into practice, we can easily allow our focal point to shift. As the threatening situations pile up, we become problem-centered, and our children fall into third or fourth place on the priority list.

Through painful experience I finally learned that my emotional temperament does not allow me to fight on the activism battlefield without confusing priorities. Whenever I try to function there, my whole family suffers.

I first became aware of that several years ago when contract negotiations broke down between teachers and administrators in our high school district. Teachers sent word home with the students that unless parents talked some sense into board members, they would strike.

Panic-stricken, I called a board member. She assured me that school would go on; but my panic mounted when the principal sent home letters soliciting the emergency help of parents in the event of a strike.

For the next few days I moved about in a frenzy. What more could I do? I prayed a lot of panicky prayers, always with my mind too full of ideas for action to hear any divine answers. In the process, I practically ignored the daily needs of my family. I only really listened to them when they brought me some new tidbit of information or incendiary opinion from an angry teacher.

On the morning that our ladies' prayer group met at church, I made routine preparations to attend. All the time I continued to fret over my insoluble problem. "Why did I have to get involved in this?" I asked the Lord. "I don't know anything about collective bargaining. It's a part of economics that I don't understand, and I hate it." In desperation I prayed once more, "Lord, what shall I do?"

That time I listened, and He answered. *Ask your prayer group to pray for a settlement.*

"Is that all, Lord?"

Yes, daughter, that is all for now.

"But it's so simple." I sighed, and hurried off to share my burden with the prayer group.

The next morning, news reached the classrooms that for some unknown reason the school board, that had the day before been refusing to talk, had not only talked, but had settled the issue agreeably.

I am not naive enough to believe that answers always come this way. Further, I have no idea how many parent activists were at work in this situation. Usually activism must accompany prayer; but I have decided that when personal activism demands that I sacrifice energies and attitudes due my family, I must find another way.

Through that and other difficult situations I have learned that I am no sharpshooter. My role is one of forging pruninghooks into spears, nursing the wounded, or stocking commissary shelves, thus releasing the hands of those who must fight on the front lines.

Involvement in education demands much from parents in terms of time, energy, and prayer, especially if we are going to do it right. We cannot afford to abdicate our responsibilities to anyone, be he an educator or even God Himself. It was to us, imperfect, amateur parents, that God gave the charge to "train up a child." No matter how unqualified we may feel, we can rest assured that an all-wise, all-powerful God would never give us a duty of such importance if He knew that we, together with Him, could not handle it.

NOTES

1. Francesco Cordasco, *A Brief History of Education* (Totowa, N.J.: Littlefield, Adams, 1970), p. x.
2. Paul Adkins, *PTA Today*, April 1976.
3. Margaret Mead, *The School in American Culture* (Cambridge: Harvard U. Press, 1951), p. 33.
4. Charles R. Swindoll, *You and Your Child* (Nashville: Thomas Nelson, 1977), p. 64.

2

SETTING OUR GOALS

*To know what we want in education, we must know what
we want in general, we must derive our theory of education
from our philosophy of life.*[1]

T. S. Eliot

EDUCATION IS BIG BUSINESS in America. The price tag reads over $100
billion every year. Nearly one-third of our total population is involved full-time in education. That includes students, faculty, and
miscellaneous staff and support personnel. Add thousands of part-
timers, and the figure keeps on growing.

As we stand at the foot of the hill, holding a child by the hand,
gazing in bewilderment at the "educational castle" above, we need
not let its statistical size dazzle us. We have already taken step number one in planning our battle strategy; we have identified the enemy.
Before we can make further intelligent decisions about our involvement in the battle, we need to set some goals. We can do that by
answering two important questions: (1) What is education? and (2)
What sort of child do we hope it will produce?

Contemporary theologian and book author Dr. R. C. Sproul tells
of his visit to his daughter's kindergarten parent meeting. Here the
principal talked about the children's daily schedule.

"Don't be alarmed," he said, "if your child comes home and tells
you that he was playing with puzzles or modeling clay in school.
I can assure you that everything in the daily routine is done with a
purpose."

In precise detail he explained how each moment of the day was
professionally designed to serve some specific educational purpose.
During the question period that followed, Dr. Sproul challenged the

principal: "I am deeply impressed by the careful planning that has gone into this program. I can see that everything is done with a purpose in view. My question is . . . what is the overall purpose of your purposes? In other words, what kind of a child are you trying to produce?"

After an uneasy pause, the embarrassed administrator admitted: "I don't know; no one ever asked me that question."[2]

As parents, we cannot afford to be caught with red faces, not knowing the answer to those vital quesitons. We must not be surprised if educators do not have a clear answer or one that satisfies us. Unless they share our God-centered view of life, neither will they share our educational goals. The goals of any educational system will be determined by the goals and values of the society that plans that system.

Modern secular education is the brainchild of a society in which most people "tend to worship their work, to work at their play, and to play at their worship. As a result, their meanings and values are distorted, their relationships disintegrate faster than they can keep them in repair, and their lifestyles resemble a cast of characters in search of a plot."[3] Even some Christian educators are influenced by this prevalent philosophy.

Little wonder when such a society, built on relative, materialistic values, tells us that education is merely a means to bring about self-realization, better status and an altered social structure.

What, then, is education?

Defining education is like defining love. Everybody talks about it. We all think we know what it means. But trying to put it into words is like attempting to capture a waterfall in a perfume bottle; most of it spills out around the edges. The most effective method for describing such complex subjects is to paint pictures that demonstrate the things they do and do not do.

Education does not merely teach children facts and skills so they can do things well. My child may master many facts of mathematics, science, and history; he may learn to analyze music, art, and literature; he may develop good communication skills and a strong disciplined body. He still can be lacking in education.

For education prepares the whole person—body, mind, soul, and spirit—to function with consistent maturity in a fragmented world. That goes beyond training a child to *do* some things; it prepares him to *be* something as well. "Children are not things to be molded, but people to be unfolded."[4]

God has built into each child a complex system of potential for growth into a totally unique adult person, prepared to fulfill His perfect plan. When we recall our instruction to "train up a child in the way he should go" (Proverbs 22:6), we assume that applies to indoctrinating the child with our moral and spiritual values. But no matter how basic that is, it is only a beginning. In this verse, God is urging us to help develop the child's total latent, individual person.

Each of our little charges has a body through which he receives stimuli from the outside world and interacts with it. He has a mind in which he interprets the input received through bodily senses. He also has a soul and a spirit. Although Bible scholars disagree about the distinction between soul and spirit, for our purposes we shall divide them in this way. The *soul* is the seat of a child's moral and emotional self, and the *spirit* is that part of his inner being with which he relates to God.

How does the education process help the child to unfold his complex person in all of those areas?

First, education develops the child's mind. That is done by the transmission of culture through what we call *general education*. When I was a child, I went to school to fill my mind with the three Rs, science, and history. From my childish viewpoint, the music that I loved and the physical education and art that I detested had nothing to do with making me educated. Today I know that all of those things fall into the category of general education.

I have discovered that general education also teaches the child to reason. Above all, it teaches him to ask why—to search beneath the surface of life's phenomena and find the deep reasons for everything.

Some parents are threatened or irritated by a child's why's. In his famous novel *Great Expectations*, Charles Dickens depicts a scene that demonstrates that attitude and its effect on the child. Pip, the young orphan boy, asks his married sister guardian an endless array of questions. For the moment, his questions center on an escaped convict with whom he has just had a chance secret encounter. Finally, exasperated, the sister turns to the boy and philosophizes about criminals in general:

"They murder, they rob and forge and do all sorts of bad; and they always begin by asking questions."

The boy promptly slinks off to bed, certain he must be headed for a life of crime simply because he asks too many questions.

A child's questioning nature is a precious and fragile gift from God. Without it, how would he learn? While a good education must impart wisdom, it must also nurture inquisitiveness so that the child learns how to go on learning and expanding his horizons for the rest of his life.

Not only does education culture a child's mind; it also involves his body. The educated body must be disciplined in skills to prepare the emerging adult to function in a competitive world.

Even the ancient Hebrews, whose entire educational system was built on the teaching of the Mosaic law, set vocational training at the top of their priority lists. Boys worked with their fathers to learn a useful trade. Girls learned essential domestic skills from their mothers.

Modern educators do not always consider the need for vocational preparedness as carefully as they ought. A couple of years ago I worked as a classroom aide with a group of high school juniors and seniors. One boy wrote an essay in which he pictured a graduate about to receive a diploma, feeling unprepared to leave the system and face life on his own.

"There is no telling what will become of him," the boy wrote. "School doesn't teach him what he needs to know after he graduates. He knows what has happened one hundred or two hundred years ago, but a lot of good that's going to do him now."

Any kind of education that does not relate past events to present problems and show how general education and physical training can be useful in acquiring living skills will leave our children, like this boy, stranded on the shores of adulthood. An effective system of education strikes a balance between general education, physical conditioning, and vocational training.

A third area in which education develops the child's whole person is the soul, or his emotional and moral self. Educating the soul means majoring on the sort of disciplined moral training that produces strong character. Theodore Roosevelt once said, "To train a man in mind and not in morals is to train a menace to society."[5] Similarly, to train a child in vocational skills and not help him develop moral character traits based on biblical values prepares him to function as a materialistic machine.

Emotional maturity too is important here. We all expect a young child to be self-centered and not able to control his emotions. But we are terribly disappointed when our efforts at educating him fail to help him get rid of those childish characteristics. Until he learns to overcome them, he is emotionally unprepared for adult life.

Finally, a complete education addresses itself to the needs of the child's spirit. Each child is capable of relating to God and fellowshipping with Him, but the spirit is like the mind, body, and soul. It needs nurturing, instruction, and guidance if it is to realize its great potential. A child left to himself in the area of spiritual education will live by the dictates of his sinful human nature and never know fellowship with God. That is why the Scriptures consistently stress the importance of parents' sharing biblical truth with their children (see Deuteronomy 6:1-9, Psalm 78:1-7, and Ephesians 6:4).

One thing needs to be clarified, however. Spiritual training does not automatically guarantee the success of the total education process. In a prayer meeting, I once heard a woman share her burden for the high school students on her block. "They think what they need to do is to find themeslves," she lamented. "I just want to get hold of them and tell them that all they need to do is to find Jesus."

Immediately her words took me back to my youth. In those days I had been convinced that all I needed was a strong spiritual base. Everything else seemed superfluous. Surely I knew who I was, where I was going, and how I was going to get there. I would not admit to having any problems that could be solved by educating either the mind, the body, or the soul. To me, that meant admitting that my Christianity was not adequate. Sure of my own position, convinced that no vocation in life was God-pleasing except a full-time Christian service career, conforming to all I was taught in church, asking no questions, I became what one writer calls a "safe, sensible person . . . a contradiction in terms, a faded replica of the man in Christ, ill defined around the edges."[6]

When I began raising a family, I carried my spiritually exclusive philosophy with me. I saturated the minds of my children with biblical truth but practically ignored some of the other facets of their personalities. God was gracious to us all. He gave me a husband who had the wisdom to help balance my extreme positions. Furthermore, He did not give us meek, submissive, little, rubber-stamp off-spring. Instead He gave us three spunky children who tugged away at the fringes of my monastic attitudes until they finally helped me see that we were all total persons—not just embodied spirits.

What is *education?* Broadly and briefly we have defined it as "the preparation of the whole person—body, mind, soul, and spirit—to function with consistent maturity in a fragmented world." It consists of a balanced training in all the areas, with no one area over-emphasized (note Luke 2:52, where Jesus provides the perfect example of balanced education in a child).

What sort of a child do we hope education will produce? How you answer that question will depend upon what is important to you and to your child. To help you to decide, try the following exercise. Take three pieces of paper and jot down these things:

Sheet #1: What are your personal and family values? What do you consider important? Number items on your list in order of priority.

Sheet #2: List characteristics of your child—his temperament, attitudes, interests, talents, apparent academic strengths and weaknesses, special aptitudes.

Sheet #3: Based realistically on facts and observations on the first two sheets, begin listing the things that you hope your child's education will accomplish. Be sure to include all you hope he learns, not just those things he gets at school.

Your goal listing will consist of both general and specific things. If your child is quite young yet, be prepared for his so-far-unrevealed characteristics to change some of the goals you are setting today. Most important of all, do not consider this list a rigid standard that your child must be forced to live up to. It is only a guideline to help you to help him reach his potential. Do not chisel it in marble. Write it lightly in pencil and keep an eraser handy.

For starters, here is a list of the general accomplishments that we should all expect from an education that makes a child a well-rounded, mature person. The list assumes that your child has average academic potential.

1. It teaches him to read. In addition, it enables him to enjoy reading, to interpret what he reads, to read critically and widely in order to broaden his horizons.

2. It teaches him math facts and computation skills, but also how

to balance a checkbook, figure a 15 percent discount, cut a recipe in half, and compute gas mileage. The mastery of math skills familiarizes a child with the patterns and relationships built into his universe by his Creator.

3. It teaches him to write a grammatically sound, understandable sentence, but also to write with depth of thought.

4. It teaches him the basic facts of science. It also leads him to practice good health habits, enjoy animals and scenic wonders, and ask a never-ending stream of questions about the natural world around him.

5. It teaches him the facts of history. It also helps him to understand such things as how world events have affected our society and prepared us for what it is today (e.g., how conditions before the fall of Rome parallel conditions in modern Western civilization and why we can all be proud of our national and cultural heritage).

6. It teaches him the meaning of good art, drama, and music. It also leads him to appreciate and enjoy those things, either as a participant or a spectator.

7. It teaches him the value and functions of his body. It also motivates him to keep in shape by exercise, good nutrition, proper rest, and good work habits.

8. It helps him to master certain vocational skills. It also teaches him to enjoy his work as a gift from God, to work to the best of his ability, and to cooperate with fellow workers.

9. It helps him to develop his talents, but also to accept himself and other talented persons without either egotistical pride, inferiority, or jealousy.

10. It teaches him the value of honesty, chastity, good human relations, self-control and creativity. It also leads him to depend upon the power of God and the exercise of self-discipline to work out godly virtues in daily life.

11. It enables him to know his Bible from cover to cover, but also to worship, and to commit himself to the God of that Bible without reservation.

"Maturity is the accomplishment of years," wrote Jim Elliot.[7] We must not be discouraged when the sort of child that we hope education will produce does not appear at the high school or college commencement. That event simply will mark what the word indicates—a beginning. Education is, after all, a lifetime affair.

When the day comes, we must let loose of that trusting hand and wave to the young adult setting off on his own. If education has done its job, we can be assured that the seeds of maturity have been planted, watered, and sprouted into healthy seedlings. For the ultimate in hope insurance, we know that the God who has guided us through the planting years goes along to cultivate and nurture the seedling and bring it to a full and beautiful maturity.

NOTES

1. T. S. Eliot, "Modern Education and the Classics," cited by Robert M. Hutchins, "The Great Anti-School Campaign," in *The Great Ideas Today, 1972* (Chicago: Encyclopaedia Britannica, 1972), p. 452.
2. R. C. Sproul, *Knowing Scripture* (Downers Grove, Ill.: Inter-Varsity, 1977), pp. 25-26.
3. Gordon Dahl, *Work, Play, & Worship* (Minneapolis: Augsburg, 1972).
4. Source unknown.
5. Paul Kienel, *Reasons for Sending Your Child to a Christian School* (La Habra, Calif.: PK Books, 1978), p. 100.
6. Eileen Guder, *God, But I'm Bored* (Garden City, N.Y.: Doubleday, 1971), p. 53.
7. Elisabeth Elliot, *Shadow of the Almighty* (N.Y.: Harper & Row, 1958), p. 91.

3

PLAYING OUR ROLES

Our ground is good, and we work it to the utmost, but our chief ambition is for the education of our children.[1]

Josephus

MARK TWAIN once said, "Education is what you must acquire without any interference from your schooling."

A bit of an exaggeration, to be sure, but his words reflect a sound educational principle—namely, that most of our children's education takes place outside of the school classroom. It happens on the patio, as we sit sipping colored-water "tea" with a six-year-old; on the front lawn, as the whole family declares war on a healthy crop of burr clover; in a Sunday morning worship service; around the daily dinner table; at the shopping mall ten days before Christmas; in the family automobile headed for the dentist; on the neighborhood baseball field; before the television set; on a high mountain trail in the midst of a backpacking adventure; at the annual family reunion; at Grandpa's funeral service.

In the days when ours was a simple agricultural society, the home provided most of the basic educational needs of its children, with some assistance from the church. But times have changed.

We live in a day of specialization where all of life is compartmentalized. We have a separate cubbyhole for everything—vocation, religion, social relationships, recreation, education, and on down the line. Conveniently, the church is available to take care of our religious cubbyhole, and the "castle on the hill" handles all our child's educational needs. That efficient arrangement frees parents to give undivided attention to all the other cubbyholes. Right? Wrong!

Many successful, well-educated parents have practiced this approach. But when their children faced important milestones, tragedy sometimes resulted. Some have failed to get high school diplomas, driver's licenses, even jobs. The reason? They could not read well enough to meet the requirements.

Always the pattern was the same—an outraged parent would point an accusing finger at the "rotten school system." Indeed, something is lacking in those systems that let a child reach his teens without learning to read, but what sort of parental neglect would allow a child to reach his late teens without finding out that he could not read?

In today's society, not just one but three major institutions contribute to the education of the child—the school, the church, and the home. Only two, the home and the church, were ordained of God. The third, the school, was established by man to accomplish those things that the first two were either unable or unwilling to do. In this chapter we will look briefly at all three institutions and consider what specific role each plays in helping to reach the educational goals that we have set for our children.

Obviously, the home is the child's first schoolroom. Here he learns to smile, to talk, to tie his shoes. He also learns responsibility and a system of values and morals. Most parents would agree that, in addition, they must begin the child's general education, skills training, and spiritual training.

We sometimes forget that this primary learning continues to be the responsibility of the home. For some things, we can delegate the direct responsibility to outsiders. Professional educators are generally more qualified than we are to give our children the bulk of their general education. The same may be true of most skills training. My son is planning a law career. If my husband and I had to impart to him all his education, he never would pass the bar exam. We have delegated that responsibility to a trustworthy university. At the same time, if we did not investigate the university, or if we did not do all we could to see that our son was prepared intellectually, morally, and spiritually for university life, then we would have failed in our parental duty.

Some areas of education cannot be so simply delegated to the school. Many parents are upset by the Supreme Court ruling against mandatory Scripture reading and prayer in schools. This does not particularly distress me. For one thing, what the ruling says and what we have been led to believe it says are often two different things. We will discuss this in a later chapter. Most important, the religious training of my children is *my* duty. I see it as a privilege far too sacred to share with or abdicate to some schoolteacher who may have no personal faith and may even use the Scripture reading/ prayer time as an opportunity to ridicule God and His Word.

Sex education is another family kind of responsibility, which we may or may not want to share with the school. My own district maintains (or at least they did while my children were in elementary school) quite a conservative program which begins at the upper elementary levels and is optional. By law, materials must be open for parental review. According to district policy, when children ask moral or technical questions of an intimate nature, they are told: "Those are family questions. Ask your parents about them." My husband and I have examined the programs and materials and seen no reason to object to anything. At the same time, we have prepared our children to handle the information they have received in such classes by instilling our own Christian moral values into their thinking.

Perhaps you live in a district where ultraliberal sex education programs exist. You have both good reason and strong obligation to speak up. Investigate your situation; make your wishes known. Basically, sex education is a family matter. Only you, the watchful parent, can insure that you maintain control over it.

Someone has estimated that the school has our children 16 percent of the time, and the church only 1 percent. But the home still has responsibility for the child 83 percent of the time. Little wonder then that many studies have found that the major factor in determining a child's academic performance is not the school, the teachers, or the curriculum, but the home background of the child.

That does not imply that the school and the church have no role to play. No matter how great our parental responsibilities or opportunities, we cannot do the job alone. We do need help from both the school and the church. How much can we expect the school to accomplish?

The Chinese have a proverb that sounds like a distant echo of modern thinking: "If a man commits a crime, punish his schoolmaster." To the Chinese, the word *schoolmaster* was a figure of speech referring to all persons responsible for a child's training. In our compartmentalized society, however, we have often applied this literally and have become guilty of an unrealistic type of educational buck-passing. We have pawned off onto the schools a whole raft of educational responsibilities that our great-grandparents would never have allowed the school even to talk about. In the good old days, school was the place to learn the three Rs, respect for cultural and national heritage, and specialized vocational skills—all things that parents were unequipped to teach.

Modern schools are expected, in addition, to provide free meals, recreation, counseling, and babysitting services. They are asked to teach nutrition, health habits, discipline, respect for others and oneself, bicycle and driving safety, sex education, values, manners, and decision-making skills. They are called upon to solve social problems that the community has failed to solve at the adult level—segregation, violence, drug abuse, political graft, crime.

We recognize many of those as functions that the home ought to be performing. What then can we expect of the schools?

The teaching of the three Rs? Certainly! If my child fails to learn to read, write, or compute at school, what then? I must go find out why. It may mean that I will have to get involved personally in solving the problem. Most tough learning problems can be solved only by parent/school teamwork.

Our oldest started school in a Dutch kindergarten while my husband served a tour of military duty in the Netherlands. She spent the first month of grade one in an Air Force school just before we returned to the United States. For the next month we were traveling enroute to our new assignment. In November she enrolled in a stateside school. Her military teacher had assured us that she would encounter no difficulties.

"They don't really get down to work for the first two months," she told us.

But that teacher did not know the school our daughter was to attend. She was lost. Classmates were already reading, and she hardly knew the letters of the alphabet. If I had known then what I know now, I could have taught her many things myself and prepared her for the adjustment.

On the third day, I went to school for a conference with the teacher. The frustrated teacher's news for me (within the child's hearing range) was: "This girl is so far behind she will never catch up."

Stunned and unbelieving, I suggested, "Why not let her parents give it a try?"

I went home that day with an armload of ditto sheets. During the weeks that followed, our daughter spent two hours each evening with her daddy and the dittos. Patiently, he drilled her on phonics and explained mathematical principles, using toy blocks.

Within a few weeks she had nearly caught up with her peers. By the beginning of the next school year, she was promoted into the top reading group. Ten years later, she graduated with honors in the top 5 percent of her high school class.

I have talked with several mothers who taught their own children to read when the school's reading program was not adequate for them. One mother said that she used to send her children to bed half an hour early. "You can have the light on and read a book for half an hour," she told them. It worked wonders—not only in getting them to bed on time but also in motivating them to learn to read well.

Is the teaching of the three Rs the limit of a school's obligation? What about morals and social skills? What about respect for cultural and national heritage?

Those are difficult questions. Our modern society is based on pluralism, which means that every man, woman, and child is considered to be free to live by his own value system. No longer do the citizens of our country agree about the excellence of a biblically-based system of morals and ethics. When a non-Christian school teaches one set of moral values, parents who disagree may complain loudly. The teacher gets caught in the middle. The answer has been an attempt to ignore the teaching of morals completely. It is impossible! Every teacher, either consciously or unconsciously, communicates her own moral values and attitudes toward social problems and cultural heritage. Often the values she models wield more powerful influence on her students than the things she teaches formally. Unfortunately, some of the leaders in education who have been responsible for establishing educational trends, have attempted to use the school system as a tool for promoting their own atheistic, materialistic values.

For those reasons, many Christian parents are electing to place their children in Christian day schools, which share the responsibility for training in strong Christian morals. Those who leave their children in public or non-Christian private schools soon learn that they cannot expect the school to handle this area of education. The most they can ask and pray for is that the school at least will not destroy the moral principles that they have built into their children at home and in the church.

While we are reminding ourselves that the school's role is limited, we need to apply the same rules to the church. If the school cannot handle the job of providing my child's general education without my preparation, support, assistance, and monitoring, then certainly I should not expect the church to give him all the spiritual training he will need for life.

Of the two God-established institutions, only the home is instructed in the Bible to educate children. Old Testament parents taught their children by use of Hebrew religious rituals, by direct instruction, and by example. The early church strongly favored home-based education. William Barclay has summarized the consensus of early church opinion on the subject as follows: "It is the parent who is responsible for bringing the child into the world; and it is the parent who is responsible for bringing the child to God. The child is the gift of God to the parent, and the child must be the gift of the parent to God."[2]

What then can we ask of the church (see Appendix 1)? The possibilities of Christian education are limitless. Perhaps your church offers so many programs that after your child has attended everything open to him, you cannot imagine what more is left for you to teach him. More likely, there is no time left for you to do anything with him. I have been in churches like that and found them threatening for two reasons.

First, they absorbed all of my children's time. Second, they absorbed far too much of my own time—not just as chauffeur but as adult leader in many of the programs. As a result, none of us had either time or energy to concentrate on making the home a center for learning.

That does not have to happen, however. The church has a God-given obligation to supplement and support the home, but never to compete with it.

One church in our community sees the family as the number one priority in its Christian education program. "It is simply our duty to assist parents in doing the job," says the Christian education pastor.

In practice that means that the pastor and staff concentrate on training parents to teach their own children. Parents of high school young people meet regularly with their youth sponsors to review current problems and plans. Always they are reminded: "If anything on this calendar conflicts with family plans or seems too much for you

or your teenagers to handle, we expect you to limit their participation."

That church insists that a volunteer for Christian education service
consult with his whole family before assuming any responsibilities.
They encourage husband/wife teaching teams. When a parent ad-
mits that he must choose between teaching a Sunday school class and
serving as a school classroom aide, the answer is an unhesitating:
"God will provide other people with different priorities for this Sunday school class. You go and help where you will touch your own
children's lives."

In a number of ways the church can become directly involved in
community education and youth evangelism. That may take the form
of training and supporting teachers of release time and home Bible
classes. Many churches establish their own Christian day schools. I
met one young scientist who goes into the public schools and gives
up-to-date lectures in which he relates scientific and economic topics
to biblical truth. Other organizations sponsor lectures and public
forums on school campuses (see Resource List). I have heard of one
community where parents and churches objected to a sex education
program that had been adopted by their school board. As a result,
when the board selected a committee to revise the objections out of
the program, they included Christian parents and local ministers. I
have also heard of one church in the Midwest that is sponsoring
music lessons and a band in a community where the music program
at school fell victim to budget cuts.

The most important work the church will ever do is to encourage
and equip parents to join ranks in the Army for Quality Education.
That brings us back to the role of the home. There are four ways that
parents can work with the local church to assure that it is able to
function adequately:

1. Take our own job seriously and assume our role as primary spiritual trainers of our children.

2. Support the Christian education programs of our churches with
prayer and help as guided by the Holy Spirit and agreed upon by the
whole family.

3. Teach our children to ask questions and think through the things
they hear in church and Sunday school. Encourage them to ask a
teacher, "Why?" when he does not offer reasons or biblical docu-
mentation for statements he makes.

4. Demand quality in Christian education. Often we accuse the

public schools of doing a poor job in teaching basic skills. At the same time we seldom inquire to see whether our churches are doing any better in biblical education.

During our son's senior year in high school, he told me: "You know, Mom, I really didn't learn very much in Sunday school through the years. We just heard the same Bible stories repeated over and over, and you had already taught me all of those at home."

"But didn't you learn how to apply biblical truth to daily life?" I asked.

"Oh, sure!" he answered. "Don't lie! Don't cheat! Don't steal! All the great sins of little kids. But I didn't have any problems with those things anyway, so it didn't mean that much to me. What I need now are some classes that make me think through what I already know and help me know why I believe what I believe—the kinds of things you've been teaching me—something to prepare me for what I'll hear at the university."

I wept inside as I realized that I had let my son down. All those years I had struggled, sometimes with very little cooperation or response, to motivate and challenge teachers in teacher training classes in the small churches we had attended. But in the process of our own busyness, my husband and I had not seen the urgency of searching long and hard enough to find a church where the Christian education department was committed to excellence and provided the depth of teaching our son needed to supplement what we gave him at home.

Education is a cooperative battle, a team effort involving professional educators, church workers, and parents, each playing his God-given role. The job will only get done when we parents sort out the roles of the platoon recruits, set realistic expectations for each one, and assume full responsibility for our positions as regiment commanders.

NOTES

1. Josephus, *Against Apion* I. 12, cited in William Barclay, *Educational Ideals in the Ancient World* (Grand Rapids: Baker, 1959), p. 12.
2. Ibid., p. 262.

4

GETTING READY FOR SCHOOL

The most effective way to foster a preschool child's intellectual and educational development is to ensure the high quality of his in-home experiences—verbal, educational, emotional, kinetic, and artistic.[1]

Paul Copperman

WHEN I WAS IN THIRD GRADE, I overheard Grandma telling my mother about my younger cousin, "She's had her tonsils out, so now she's ready to start school."

How strange! I had never had my tonsils out. Yet I had started school three years earlier, and I was doing fine. As far as I knew, all my mother did to get me ready for school was to make me a new dress and buy me some new shoes, a lunch pail, and a box of crayons. Many years later, as I studied child psychology and taught Sunday school classes, I began to realize that preparing a child for school meant more than tonsillectomies, sewing sprees, and shopping trips. Not until I became a parent did I fully realize how complex the process could be.

Preparing a child for school, I discovered, begins by preparing ourselves for parenthood. We need to learn all we can about children and how they learn and about the educational system to which we entrust them. As one teacher told me, "a parent can't learn too much."

How do children learn? By being lectured? By having their knuckles rapped when they misbehave? By rote memorization techniques? By sitting silently while adults talk around and above their heads? Some generations have believed those to be the only effective methods of educating children. Today we know that children

39

learn in a variety of ways. In this chapter we will mention five of those ways and discuss how we can nurture the atmosphere conducive to such learning.

First, learning begins with personal acceptance and the building of strong, warm, approving relationships at home. Almost instinctively, well-adjusted parents know that newborn babies need a sense of warmth and sheltered approval. Who can help loving a fresh bundle from heaven, enveloped in sweet softness and baby-velvet skin?

But what happens when the sweetness turns to obstinancy, and the beauty disappears into gangly awkwardness? If anything, the child's need for that same warm affirmation intensifies at that point. How to give it then takes conscious effort and discipline, along with more than a little prayer.

Both accepting our children and building solid relationships with them involve the use of good communication skills. Talking on the eyeball-to-eyeball level with small children suggests, "Let's be friends." Listening with attentive ears, open hearts, and no strings attached says: "You are special and more important to me than I can tell you." Resisting the urge to interrupt a child, hog a conversation, or demonstrate attitudes of superiority—all of those are tested techniques of constructive communication with children.

Pouring on the deserved compliments while minimizing criticisms goes a long way toward teaching a child to like himself. It can also show him the essential truth that failure is not fatal but only a temporary stepping-stone enroute to learning and success. One couple shared with me their successful formula for criticism and praise. "We determined early in our parenting," they said, "never to criticize our children in front of anyone else, and at least fifty percent of our boasting about them, we must do in their presence."

"There is nothing so powerful as a second-hand compliment," one teacher told me. "Tell someone else, in the child's presence, how pleased you are with the child's progress, and he will glow all over. It's a tremendous boost to self-esteem."

These things become especially important when a child must repeat a grade in school. Many parents do not understand that grade retention is often the best possible thing that can happen to many children. We want our children to make us proud. We panic when they appear to be failing to reach the top levels of performance we expect of them. We have to deal with our own feelings quickly in such cases to keep from blaming the child, who already is smarting under the pain of a failure stigma. If we can truly believe that, for our child, this retention is the most effective tool to insure his ultimate success, we can help him to eradicate all those stigmatized images and make the most creative possible use of his difficulty.

When a child goes off to school, he will need all the well-balanced self-esteem that we can help him develop. He is going to face a hostile world that often has little time to listen to either his words or his heartbeats. We want him always to feel confident that his home is a safe haven for a wounded spirit.

A second way that children learn is through exposure. If I show my child *National Geographic,* give him pets, and take him on visits to the zoo, he learns to love animals. If I let him assist in decorating the house during Advent with works of quality Christmas art and take the time to explain to him the meaning of each piece, he grows up learning to appreciate good art. If I take him on mountain hiking trips, he learns to love the out-of-doors and to identify poison oak or poison ivy. If I read to him often and let him see me reading for my own pleasure, he is ready and eager to learn to read for himself. If I let him make collections of rare treasures—rocks, feathers, or postage stamps—he is prepared to learn about rocks, birds, and other nations and cultures. If I take him to church and Sunday school, not only will his faith be strengthened, he will also learn to meet people and interact with them.

"A space of time is given each person to know, absorb, enjoy and share life," writes one Christian education specialist. "Part of our gift to our pupils is to see that they miss as little of the wonders of life as possible."[2] What a challenge for educational parenting!

One pastor I interviewed told how he and his wife have established some family traditions of exposure. One Monday morning, because it was his day off, he invited his children to jump into bed with him. As the three little ones wriggled in under the covers, each clamoring for the lion's share of his hugs and attention, the father began to tell them a story. "It was totally extemporaneous and probably not terribly well composed," he recalls. But it delighted his children. The next Monday morning, almost as if on a predetermined cue, all three youngsters bounded into bed with their father once more. "Tell us another story," they pleaded.

Now they would not miss a Monday morning story hour. In the meantime, the mother spends hours each week in the public and school libraries, choosing books to enjoy at home. The two older children, now in school, are reading their own books and loving the experience as they share their reactions with the parents.

As we attempt to increase a child's exposure to his world and to new ideas, we need to exercise special caution in our use of television. When it is properly used, it can serve as our strong ally. Without close selectivity, parental supervision, and strict time limits, however, it can become our enemy's number one weapon. We all know that much of television attacks and erodes the values we are trying to inculcate in our homes, but it does other dangerous things as well.

Paul Copperman, in his book *The Literary Hoax,* mentions two of the subtle problems with television. "Television's effect on children is to create an expectation that learning should be easy, passive, and entertaining. They judge their teachers by the entertainment standards of television. . . . Most damaging is the sense of knowledge and sophistication which young people acquire from extensive exposure to a medium which attempts to convince its audience that its programs have depth and significance, when in truth most information children acquire from television is so superficial and discontinuous as to have little value."[3]

Television has tremendous power to destroy creativity and initiative. Unlike a good book, which stimulates the imagination, the fast-paced, always moving screen eliminates both the need and the time for such mental activity. When a child spends several hours a day passively watching other people solving problems and having adventures, that becomes a substitute for the problem-solving and adventures he needs to be having for himself. Even those children's programs designed especially to teach preschoolers living skills and stimulate their creativity are highly suspect of killing creativity in many children. They can also rob parents of many of the special opportunities for getting acquainted with their children, as they assume many of the teaching roles normally reserved for parents.

Of course, a trip to the zoo takes a lot more of Mom's and Dad's time and effort than turning on the television to watch an animal show. Besides, the zoo probably does not have as many rare animals as television can display. Perhaps television can provide a good background of information and enthusiasm for a family outing. But what television program can substitute for the genuine thrills of throwing fish to the seals or petting a llama or watching two tiger kittens romping close by, or craning one's tiny neck to catch a glimpse of a giraffe's face and twitching ears? In what way do television's cold, on/off button and recorded voice substitute for the warmth of a parent's hand and the music of his voice as the family shares this special experience (see Appendix 3)?

If we want our children to get the most out of their years of formal schooling, we need to begin at birth to set a pattern of guided exposure to real-life persons, places, skills, hobbies, reading materials, cultural pursuits, ideas, and attitudes. That prepares them by stimulating their curiosity and arousing their enthusiasm for learning. It also prevents much of the panicky trauma many overprotected, underexposed children experience on their first venture out of the nest into the classroom.

Third, children learn by doing. How quickly they begin to grab a spoon and say, "Do it self, Mommy." Children are born with a high degree of creativity. The parent who is afraid to take the risk of letting his child do things for himself will destroy that fragile gift of creativity. In the process he will build into the child some unreasonable fears of personal failure and of the world around him.

Growth in our children happens when we give priority to sharing our lives by doing things together. The young child especially learns by using all his senses. We can help him most by providing abundant opportunities for him to taste, smell, hear, see, and touch his way through the preschool years. We also encourage growth by giving him household responsibilities—letting him help fix dinner, wash the dishes, follow Daddy under the family car and hand him the wrenches, make his own bed, and pick cans of soup off the grocery shelf. We need to take special care in choosing toys and games that allow for a maximum of personal involvement and development of both motor, creative, and thinking skills. By encouraging the child to take part in family worship, we prepare him to share more freely with his peers when he starts school.

The fourth way that children learn is by guidance. It has been said that the way to handle an active child is simply to "wiggle him in the right direction."[4] We can accomplish this in two basic ways: by example and by discipline.

Nothing is more powerful in the life of a child than the influence of parental example. Earl Butz, former US secretary of agriculture, paid this enviable tribute to his father: "Seldom a day passes that I don't pull something useful, something philosophical, something inspirational from my association with that wonderful man. For this heritage, I am eternally grateful."[5]

The magazines we read, the jokes we laugh at, the way we react to a meddlesome neighbor, how we respect traffic lights and speed laws in solitary places, our attitudes toward work, our treatment of our spouses, our readiness to admit to faults and to having more questions than answers on some issues, evidences of where we place our values, how we talk about others, whether or not we are continuing to grow and learn new things—all of those and a million more details of daily living in the intimacy of the home provide clear influential guidance for our children. One parent told me that she prepares her children to face moral, social, philosophical, and educational problems by "example more than anything else. I know my own way of dealing with things rubs off." Everything we do as parents demonstrates and supports our view of life—whether God's viewpoint or that of our man-sufficient world.

Eugenia Price, in her book *Woman To Woman*, states that every child has an urgent psychological need to be proud of his parents. Somehow his own self-esteem is tied up with his parents' good behavior.[6] As I mulled that one over, I began to realize that my conduct not only provides a pattern for my children, but it also helps them develop social and emotional maturity.

Today we hear a lot about discipline, particularly in the classroom. It is so easy to lay all the blame for lack of discipline on the school system. But we must realize that discipline begins at home. We can prepare our children for a life of cooperation with education and all of society by providing them with the solid guidance accorded by consistent, loving discipline. One psychologist/consultant told a conference of teachers, "If you're good at discipline, you can thank your parents, because they modeled discipline management principles for you."[7]

Finally, children learn through direct instruction. Usually we put this method first on the list when we think of teaching children. Unless a child feels acceptance, enjoys exposure to expanding experiences, is allowed to do new things, and receives guidance from positive examples and consistent discipline, no amount of telling him what to do or how to feel will accomplish a thing. I like the way our family pastor defines a teachable moment. "It is that moment when the child says: 'I've seen you live the life; now I want to know why.' "[8]

During the first four years of a child's life his parents teach him well over half of all the things they will ever teach him. When I first heard that, I did not believe it. I began to count up all the lessons of mind, emotions, and spirit as well as the shoe-tying, spoon-handling, walking, and talking kinds of things. I finally stopped short and admitted that the figures must be accurate. Many of those things must be taught by direct instruction, often "line upon line, and precept upon precept" (Isaiah 28:10), a consistent drilling coupled with modeling in order to communicate thousands of basic living skills.

In interviewing teachers I learned that a surprising number of parents neglect to teach simple good health habits. "Tell the parents," one teacher told me, "that in their preschool instruction program they must stress hygiene, proper nutrition, sufficient sleep, and exercise."

The most important subjects we teach our children are those that establish values and orient their minds to the God-centered world view.

Today many educators in public schools are teaching what is called "values education" or "values clarification." This practice has come about at least in part as an attempt to fill the vacuum created when religious training was thrown out of the classrooms. Teachers discovered that it is impossible to teach information and keep order without teaching morals in some form. Also, increasingly over the years children are coming from homes where they receive little or no moral training of any responsible sort.

Many Christians are alarmed by the use of these tools. If the teacher comes from a godless moral position she will very likely lead her class in the same direction. Or if, as often happens, children are left on their own to decide moral issues through group consensus techniques, the results in peer pressure can be catastrophic to young, impressionable minds.

The most effective way to teach godly values is to live them at home. But we need to give direct instruction as well. When a child acts selfishly, we can remind him of Samson and the unhappy results of his selfishness or of Dorcas and the happiness she brought to many through her unselfishness. We can question him and lead him to state for himself God's way of handling the situation. One father told me that his son was reading Mark Twain. "I've taught him to look at all the problems that people encounter in those books and ask: 'How could this person have prevented or solved his problem by following God's plan for doing things?'"

As Christian parents, we know that our clear responsibility is to instruct our children in spiritual matters. But, I think, we need to go one step further. Before we send our children out into the big, educational world, we need to do some solid research to find out what false philosophies they will be exposed to out there.

Perhaps the first thing to learn about is modern, secular humanism. Many devout church people are confused by the word *humanism*. They equate it with a warm, Christian humanitarianism or a faith in man's innate abilities, both of which draw on some potential for good, resident in every human being. But the humanistic philosophy that threatens much of education (and all of society) today is not godly in any sense of the word. Rather, it comes from the camp of the American Humanist Society, a materialistic, nonprofit religious organization whose basic doctrinal statement (the Humanist Manifesto) promotes the following views:

1. There is no God, no sin, no heaven or hell, no validity to prayer, no need for salvation, no supernatural, and no absolute truth.

2. Man is the center of his own life and master of his fate.

3. All values are relative, to be established by human experience and consensus of group opinions.

4. The goal of life is present satisfaction and realization of the full potential of the human personality, leading to a one-world society under the leadership of liberated (i.e., man-centered) man.

As you study more about secular humanism (see Resource List), it is important to recognize one thing. The modern humanist is not necessarily, as many believe, a conspirator, setting out to destroy the world. He may be a compassionate, concerned person who is desperately trying to save his world. He is probably no impassioned warmonger but a logical, thinking person. The sad thing is that his whole philosophy is built on erroneous, basic presuppositions about God and man. He will fight all our efforts to promote godliness, because he has built his whole life on an effort to support and promulgate the lie that Satan has led him to believe.

Researching these issues must be done with caution. Take special care to study the suggestions for evaluating educational materials and exposés, given at the beginning of the Resource List. Otherwise you may find yourself either sinking into hopeless depression over all the negative things you read or dashing out with a wild sword and lopping off heads that should be dealt with prayerfully and tenderly.

As we gain more information about the evil forces that oppose us and seek to influence our children, we see more clearly what basic truths we need to emphasize at home. In the beginning we need simply to show our children, by word and life, who God is and what He is like. As the child grasps those foundational truths, it is vital that we also warn him of some of the falsehoods that he will encounter in the classrooms and textbooks of his school.

When our children were little, we determined that they would never hear some convincing atheistic or humanistic line and have reason to say: "Mom and Dad hold to their old religious ideas because they have never been enlightened."

Instead, we taught them the tenets of several basic, false philosophies. By probing questions we led them to scrutinize each theory in the light of the Scriptures we had been teaching them and eventually to see the superiority of Jesus Christ and the Bible to any plan man could devise. We further warned them that all through life they would meet godless ideologies and experience pressure to follow them—hence the need for knowing their Bibles as preparation to meet the enemy. We also encouraged them to witness to and pray for the teachers who taught them errors and to let God teach them to love all the believers of error.

About a year ago I talked with a college student in our church who had recently found the Lord through the life and witness of a Christian roommate. "Even though I called myself an agnostic, I had actually been searching for God for years," he told me. "I had met a number of Christians, but they never were able to tell me why they believed in God. If just once some Christian had stood up in a science class and explained to the teacher and the class why he didn't believe in evolution, I would have begun to take Christianity seriously long before I did."

The home has been ordained of God to prepare children for their inevitable encounter with a world that is often hostile to every godly principle we hold valid and precious, but also sometimes hungry for reality and truth. I read about one Dutch university professor who held weekly discussion sessions with non-Christian university students in his home. He required his own children to attend those sessions. Although much of the talk was beyond their comprehension, they caught one clear message: God's Word is valid. And we can always bring home our own questions without fear of having to lose faith in this Book of the God of our father.[9]

Most of us cannot follow that father's pattern. But we can all dig much deeper into God's truth than we do. We can learn to use the gifts God has given us and to pass on to our children the information, wisdom, and inspiration we acquire in our growing process. None of us can excuse himself before God for not preparing his youngsters for their venture into the world of desks and textbooks. Learning to fulfill that role adequately is a vital part of every parent's battle strategy—it is one battlefield where we must all fight.

NOTES

1. Paul Copperman, *The Literary Hoax* (New York: William Morrow, 1978), p. 60.
2. Dorothy Bertolet Fritz, *Ways of Teaching* (Philadelphia: Westminster, 1965), pp. 89-90.
3. Copperman, p. 167.
4. Mack R. Douglas, *How to Make a Habit of Succeeding* (Grand Rapids: Zondervan, 1966), p. 163.
5. *Farm Journal*, June/July 1979, p. 158.
6. Eugenia Price, *Woman to Woman* (Grand Rapids: Zondervan, 1959), p. 126.
7. Fredrick C. Jones, director of Classroom Management Training Program in Santa Cruz, California, at Basic Education Leadership Conference, Santa Clara, California, November 9, 1979.
8. Paul Steele, pastor of Valley Church, Cupertino, California, May 20, 1979.
9. Linette Martin, *Hans Rookmaker: A Biography* (Downers Grove, Ill.: Inter-Varsity, 1979), pp. 121-22.

5

WHAT ARE THE ALTERNATIVES?

*Academic freedom must mean the freedom of men and
women to supervise the educational activities and aims of
the schools they oversee and support.*[1]

William F. Buckley, Jr.

THE TWO YOUNG MOTHERS at the Sunday school picnic shared a common concern with thousands of Christian parents. They had spent
five years preparing their children for the most important segment
of their pre-adult lives—the formal education experience. They had
trained them well—physically, emotionally, intellectually, and spiritually. But the prospect of entrusting these impressionable minds
and characters to the education system puzzled and frightened them.

From every source they heard ugly rumors about godless values,
physical violence, low academic standards, and teacher strikes. How
true the reports were they could not be sure, for they had not visited
the classrooms of their neighborhood schools to see firsthand what
was going on. They had not been trained to know what to look for if
they did visit.

In their newspapers they read conflicting statements:

"This country is better educating more children at all levels than
any country in the world."[2]

"For the first time, it is conceivable to envision the dismantling of
universal public, compulsory education as it has been pioneered in
America" (Professor J. Myron Atkin, dean of School of Education,
Stanford University).[3]

In the meantime the perplexed parents had friends who were very
vocal about the local Christian day school as the best solution to the
problem. "It's the only place where you can rest assured that your

51

children will receive a sound education based on godly principles and taught in a safe, supportive atmosphere." They heard that advice repeatedly.

Whom should they believe? How should they react? What choice should they make about how and where to educate their children?

Paul Copperman claims, "Parents don't want to make choices about how their children are to be educated. They want to be able to leave all those choices to a school system that they can trust."[4] That is precisely what parents have been doing, until the past few years. But the system has not always proved itself equal to that confidence. In many places it has let us down, and our children have suffered. We now know that no system that serves the public (education included) can live up to the expectations of blind, unquestioning trust. In a democracy we should never ask any system to assume absolute, unmonitored responsibility for any area of our lives.

As a result of our society's disillusionment, a rapidly growing number of parents are pulling their children out of the public school system and finding or creating alternative ways to educate them. Christian day schools! Basics schools! Parochial schools! Correspondence schools! Private schools! Never have American parents been faced with such a wide assortment of promising options from which to choose. Regardless of your situation, the choice can be very confusing. Whether your children are entering kindergarten, moving to a new community, or just needing a better quality education than they are currently receiving, you face a vitally important decision. How shall you make it?

We need to discuss the actual criteria for making such choices, but first we should look at the major options that are available and see what your child can expect to encounter with each one.

The first is the most obvious, the most popular, and probably the simplest possibility—the public school. Here Johnny will be exposed to a wide multiracial, multieconomic, multireligious mixture of children and adults. His teachers may be godly or atheistic or somewhere in between. Discipline may be strict or loose. Classrooms may be open or conventional, with or without aides. Curriculum may be basics-centered or socially oriented, closely graded or programmed to fit the child's individual pace. In December he may sing "Away in a Manger" at the annual Christmas program or "Rudolph the Red-Nosed Reindeer" in the "Winter Program."

How the local school is run and what atmosphere prevails is determined by at least five factors: (1) state and federal regulations, programs, and grants, (2) school district policies, dictated by officials and/or board members, (3) school administrators, (4) classroom teachers and aides, and (5) amount of parental and other community involvement.

One thing is certain—regardless of all the variables, parental involvement is a must. Without it, no school—public or private, Christian or secular—can be expected to complete our children's education to our satisfaction.

A second option is the parochial, or church-operated school. Parochial schools have been with us long before the public school system was an ideological twinkle in Thomas Jefferson's eye. The first schools in America were established by churches.

Today, if we send our children to parochial schools the quality of academic education they receive may vary little from what they would receive in the public school. Or the standards may be either higher or lower. Most parochial school teachers are themselves products of the public system. Even those who have studied in denominational colleges have usually been trained in many of the same educational philosophies and methods as their public school counterparts.

Overall atmosphere in parochial schools is generally more conducive to morality, discipline, and cooperation, although even here there is some variation. One thing we can usually count on in the parochial school is the inclusion in the curriculum of religious classes and/or chapel services of some sort. If the parochial school you choose for Johnny belongs to your family's church, you will probably save some tuition, and you will also have a fair idea of what sort of religious training he will receive there. Most likely, it will at least corroborate what you teach at home.

The third and most popular alternative to the public system is the Christian day school. I refer to any independent, nondenominational Christian school. Those schools are growing so rapidly in number that, in some places, their success threatens to close the public schools to all but the poor who cannot afford tuition payments. According to one estimate, two new Christian day schools open in the United States every day.[5] With open acclaim and the backing of news commentators, educators, congressmen, and Christian leaders, the Christian day school movement has become one of the most powerful forces that public education has to deal with.

Here again, the variety is wide. Most parents tend to think that all Christian schools are alike. Not so! From the Accelerated Christian Education schools (A.C.E.), where learning takes place in individual programmed texts under the guidance of supervisors who need not be certified teachers, to some of the super-traditionally structured classrooms employing methods our grandparents held to be sacred, you can find just about anything. For the most part, however, those schools do not indulge in radical educational experiments. They tend toward the more traditional side.

Some schools will put strong emphasis on patriotism, almost to the point of insisting that it is evidence of godliness. Some will operate as any other school, but with Bible classes, chapel services, and pre-class prayers tacked onto the curriculum. Others will teach all subjects by using the Bible as a corollary textbook. According to Paul Kienel, executive director of the California Association of Christian Schools, "True Christian Education teaches that the natural world takes on meaning only through the supernatural resources of God."[6] The goal of those schools is to eliminate any distinction in the students' thinking between secular and sacred truth by demonstrating how each subject is related to God and the biblical viewpoint.

Although approaches may vary, nearly all Christian day schools are striving for three things: (1) biblical, moral, and spiritual values teaching, (2) firm discipline, and (3) high academic standards.

A fourth option is the nonsectarian private school. Not all private schools are Christian. In fact, there are thousands of private, nonreligious schools in America. Those are not all exclusive boarding schools for the wealthy, preparing students for Harvard and Yale. Many kinds of private schools have been established in the past fifteen or twenty years. Almost anybody who is dissatisfied with the public system can start his own private school, providing he has the leadership capacity and the will and patience to succeed. Not that it is easy, just possible. Many educational experiments have begun in private schools (e.g., schools for the handicapped). In increasing numbers, angry parents are protesting poor quality education by starting something new and qualitatively different. In your public library, you will no doubt find books recounting success stories of those often revolutionary ventures. For a few dollars, you can even buy a paperback book called *How to Start Your Own School* (see Resource List).

Once more, be cautious. Although private education will certainly be more expensive, it does not necessarily mean more quality. Many parents have established schools because they were anxious to free their children from what they call the unhealthy and unnatural constraints of structure and absolute moral standards. In those types of schools, rote memorization, rules, and any type of educational method that cannot be labeled "fun" is usually eliminated from the curriculum. On the other hand, you may find a local private school that stands for high academic and moral standards and an old-fashioned no-nonsense approach to learning.

A fifth option, the basics school, belongs to the public school system. Called by various names—structured, formal, academics plus, fundamental, traditional, back-to-basics—it is an attempt to save the system by a return to disciplined, structured, basics-oriented education. It is interesting that their popularity with the public is serving to alert the system and make public school educators more aware of what direction they must look if they are to serve the needs and wishes of their public.

Those schools are usually instigated by tax-paying parents who insist that their children have a right to what they consider to be a better education than the local system offers without having to pay double for it. In today's climate of mistrust of the system and a strong trend to stress basic skills and raise the declining SAT* scores, the number of basics schools is mushrooming. Wherever they open their doors, they find themselves in the delightful predicament of having hundreds of children on a waiting list. Parents in one California city camped out in sleeping bags on the lawn in front of school district offices in order to be assured of a place in the classrooms when a basics school was opened in their district. By 8:00 A.M. the school was filled to capacity. The Philadelphia school system, when faced with almost five thousand applicants for admission to the one school they planned to open, opened seventeen schools instead.

Basics schools differ from community to community, depending largely on the degree of cooperation they enjoy from school boards and district officials. Some schools operate on separate campuses, often in schools that have been closed. Others coexist in the same plant beside a regular system school. Some schools are a bit narrow

*College aptitude test given to most high school seniors as a part of their college application procedure.

in their curriculum planning, omitting such courses as arts and science. Others regard the arts as one of a child's basic educational needs. Some schools receive all their funding from the local district. Others are partially funded by outside sources—parental contributions and grants of various sorts. One school I have heard about supplements the limited funds provided by a reluctant school board with monies received from a foundation created specifically for that purpose.

Most basics schools share the following distinctive features:

1. Strong emphasis on mastery of basic skills
2. Strict discipline and dress code
3. Regular homework in all classes, designed to be supervised by parents
4. Structured classroom atmosphere, usually without aides
5. Refusal to implement most federal government programs or accept their funds
6. Frequent progress reports and use of letter grades
7. Strong emphasis on good citizenship—respect, courtesy, and patriotism
8. Promotion based on achievement of grade level learning skills
9. Traditional teaching methods—e.g., mathematics drills, phonics, grammar mechanics
10. Voluntary enrollment plus parental commitment to assume a major supportive role and frequent parent/teacher conferences

Starting a basics school is no pushover. It is important for parents to be very certain that what they are asking for is really superior to that which is currently available, for the battle to obtain and maintain a basics school will often be long and difficult. Understandably, some school boards, teachers, and administrators feel threatened by the idea. They resent what they interpret as parents trying to tell them about a better way to run the schools.

At a conference on basic education, I listened to dozens of parents, teachers, and administrators tell their stories. From those stories, I concluded that parents considering this option need to begin by obtaining at least two essential things: (1) a strong force of knowledgeable, persistent parents and (2) a school board that is supportive of, or at least sympathetic to, the principle of public system supported alternative schools. Lacking those, they will have to look for some other option.

One more alternative exists—the do-it-yourself method. Some states have laws allowing parents to teach their own children at home. Laws or no laws, many parents are forced to go through lengthy and unpleasant court proceedings in order to defend what they believe is their constitutional right to do so. One writer estimates that "there are about 10,000 families now teaching their own children at home and that number is doubling every two years." He reports that the University of California is getting half a dozen applicants for admission every year who were "home educated," and they are generally very good students.[7]

Home study courses may be planned by parents who are knowledgeable and qualified to do so. Most parents who opt for the home teaching route use correspondence courses (see Resource List). In either case, parents must obtain permission from state officials to follow this option, and they usually need the counsel and assistance of a lawyer who specializes in this sort of legal proceeding. Furthermore, it appears from precedents set by many court cases that parents who request the home study option for religious reasons stand the best chance of receiving government approval.

Parents should not be too eager to try this option. Although it may sound like an easy alternative to the less-than-perfect situation you live with now, it will not be easy at all. Using correspondence and other materials to supplement classroom work may be a highly beneficial procedure. But the disadvantages of at-home schooling (social difficulties, increased work load for parents, and the possible communication of an attitude that problems are best solved by retreating from society) will often far outweigh the benefits to be derived. It is the exceptional parent indeed who can make that alternative work totally effectively.

Very likely you do not have all those options in your community, but as you search through the regiments clustered around the foot of your education hill, you may find more than you expect. Some will be assembled, active, and recruiting your help. Others may just now be forming for action, still in the tentative, struggling stages. Still others may not even be visible. The best thing you can do is to take a quick survey to discover how many specific options do exist in your individual situation.

On a separate sheet of paper or page in a notebook simply list each option available to you. Include address, phone number, type of school, name of person to contact, source from which you learned about this school, and any other immediately available information. Do not ask a lot of questions yet. That comes later. Naturally you will need to evaluate each school's philosophies, facilities, and practices in detail before you make an intelligent decision. In our next chapter we will share with you some of the questions to ask and some procedures to follow in doing such an evaluation. But for now, just get the names and addresses.

NOTES

1. William F. Buckley, Jr., *God and Man at Yale* (Chicago: Henry Regnery, 1951), p. 190.
2. *San Jose Mercury*, editorial, 5 November 1979.
3. J. Myron Atkin, *San Jose News*, 28 December 1979.
4. Paul Copperman, from speech given at Basic Education Leadership Conference, Santa Clara, California, November 8, 1979.
5. David Boehi, "The Rising Tide of Christian Education," in *Worldwide Challenge*, February 1979, p. 42.
6. Paul Kienel, *The Christian School: Why It Is Right for Your Child* (Wheaton: Scripture Press, Victor, 1974), p. 75.
7. John Holt, *LITE*, newsletter, January 1980, No. 73, p. 607.

6

CHOOSING THE BEST SCHOOL

Considering the needs of your child is the most demanding
step in finding a school.[1]

Dave Raney

FOR YEARS CHRISTIAN PARENTS have been divided over the Christian
school v. public school controversy. In literature, from church pulpits,
and over thousands of cups of coffee and telephone wires, the controversy has raged, often generating an intense amount of emotional
heat.

The two basic lines of logic being debated are represented by the
story of two couples we shall call Rob and Linda, and Bill and Melissa.

One afternoon, when her fifth grader marched through the front
door and straight to the kitchen in silence, Linda suspected trouble.
When she greeted him with, "Hi, son!" and he frowned in continued
silence, she knew there was trouble.

Suddenly the boy blurted out: "Today Miss Austin told us that the
world just happened—like a kind of accident. She said the idea of a
God was stupid!"

The mother's first reaction was panic. She was glad that her best
friend, Melissa, was not here to repeat her favorite warning: "If you
don't put your children in the Christian school, you'll one day regret
it." Linda knew Melissa would not stop there, but would go on with
the whole speech: "In a crazy world like ours, our kids desperately
need reinforcement at school for all we teach them at home. Public
schools are full of both overt and subtle influences that tear down the
authority of the home and church and destroy basic moral principles."

Linda and Rob had listened to their friends' repeated warnings
and prayerfully reevaluated the educational needs of all their chil-

61

dren. Still they believed that if they taught them well in the Scriptures at home and prayed them through the years, all would go well. After all, had God given the responsibility of moral and spiritual training to school teachers or to parents? Had He not pledged Himself to go with their children and protect their minds and hearts? The trusting parents expected their children to survive anything the schools could throw at them. Surely, they reasoned, through that sort of parent-supervised exposure to the real world, their little ones would gain strength never possible in the protected atmosphere of a Christian school. Linda and Rob were not interested in raising hothouse Christians, but tough soldiers fit for future battles in a deteriorating society.

Today, though, their theory was under fire. Maybe Bill and Melissa were right. After all, it was asking quite a bit of a child still in his formative years to stand for a faith he had not had a chance to settle for himself. Maybe he needed more time to be sheltered in the truly real world where godly viewpoints were considered the norm rather than the oddity. Were they about to regret their decision as Bill and Melissa had warned? Would that teacher persuade their son with her tools of clever logic and ridicule? And what about peer pressure? Would it finally get to him?

No way, Linda decided. *We have prepared him too well for that. He knows about the difference between evolution and creation. He also knows that his teacher is not a Christian. In fact, he has been praying for her. This could provide the opportunity for him to be the witness we have been training him to be—both to the teacher and to his classmates.*

Rob and Linda's decision was vindicated when their son assured his mother: "I can handle what Miss Austin is saying. She's not arguing with me but with the Bible. I'm just worried because I have to find a way to stop her before the rest of the class falls for her line." Several months later that same teacher began recommending that her students read some Christian books she had placed on the shelf.

"If you can read these books and still not believe in God," she explained to the class, "there is something wrong with you."

Not every public school story ends that way. Some children do succumb to teacher and peer pressure, regardless of home preparation and prayer. Some children fare much better with parents who approach the problem in the way Bill and Melissa did. They do indeed need that extra sheltering and encouragement from a Christian day school.

On the other hand, an apparently shattered faith in the fifth grade may only be a badly bruised faith that will eventually heal and become stronger for the experience. Those are the ultimate issues that no parent has any way of knowing. No one person can tell you what kind of education is best for your child. You alone can examine all the options, get acquainted with your own child, prepare him, pray the matter through to an answer, and trust the Lord with the results. In so doing, you may come out with a viewpoint slightly different from either of those we have seen. Many parents have.

Tom and Peggy have sent their children to Christian schools for what they consider the most crucial years—kindergarten, first grade, and junior high.

Jim and Susy worked hard and successfully to start a basics school in their district so they would not have to leave the public system.

In their remote community Greg and Patty found no positive solutions that they could handle. They opted for a do-it-yourself alternative, enrolling their children in a correspondence school.

As we have indicated before, every individual school situation is different. Each child is different. One observing parent told me that he put his children in two different schools. "Our daughter is in a Christian day school," he said, "because she is so susceptible to peer pressure that the public school would wipe her out. Our son is a stand-on-his-own kind of a child who needs public school exposure to build him up."

Communities differ as well. Jean and Kirk lived in a small town where no Christian school existed. No one felt the need for one. Many of the public school teachers and even the principal of one school were Christians. They held Bible studies together. Parents formed a prayer group just to pray for school needs. "God did great things there," my friend assured me.

Today the decision is more complex than it was a generation ago. Many people who once rejected the Christian school philosophy as an unnatural, sheltered escape from the real world are having second thoughts. They see that as society moves farther away from godly standards, so do the schools. There is strong evidence that in many cases the schools are being used as tools of those who want to eliminate all biblical morals from our society.

We parents are easily moved by emotional arguments that involve our children. When just the right person comes along and tells us how much danger our children are in, we may panic. As he whips out the brochures about his local alternative school, we are ready to sign up today, a move we might not necessarily make in a more logical mood or after much prayerful consideration.

Does *alternative* always mean better? Or safer? I could give you a list of parents who would give you documented reasons to answer a hearty no! Instead, let me make a few suggestions to guide you in making your own decision. If you are considering pulling your child out of a public school and seeking shelter in any one of the alternatives, ask yourself a few questions before you leave your easy chair or your knees:

1. Why do I want to think about an alternative? How bad is my present situation? Have I done all I can to make it work? How much better is the alternative I am considering? If morning chapel and a Christian faculty are the only elements that distinguish a Christian day school from my public school, I need to decide how important those two elements are.

2. What will be the immediate and long-term effects of moving my child? What will be involved in making this change? Will I be involved in court battles? Will fighting absorb all my energies so that I have none left to perform my normal parenting duties? Will the hassling injure my child more than leaving him where he is?

3. Do I expect the alternative school to do the impossible for my child? "Relying on the Christian school as a panacea is based upon the fallacy that a person can be conditioned into becoming a disciple of Jesus Christ," wrote one Christian school administrator. "There is no automatic, programmed means of insuring that a youngster will follow the Lord."[2]

Shopping for a good education is something like shopping for an automobile or a new home. Because it is a major investment, and we will live with our decision for a very long time, we need to investigate the product first-hand. It also helps to talk with other customers— people whose children already attend the school we are considering.

What should we look for in a school? Detailed answers to that question vary from family to family and student to student. Only you can determine what specific combination of ingredients is most important for each of your children. We can agree, however, that certain elements are essential if a school is to earn our respect, confidence, and support:

1. *A school must provide solid training in the basic skills.* These are the subjects that prepare a student to learn everything else that he chooses or is required to learn throughout life. Reading, writing, and arithmetic, of course, are the foundations. Most parents will agree that history, science, and the arts are also essential. A few would even insist on including foreign languages. When investigating a school, check out achievement test scores in those basic areas. See how they compare with national averages and with scores in other schools in your comunity. Are they improving or are they declining?

2. *Every school must provide an atmosphere conducive to learning.* It should include:

• facilities that are clean, warm, safe, and cheerful.

• a well-trained faculty of teachers and administrators that show their concern first for students and parents, second for each other, and finally for themselves.

• a system of effective discipline in which teachers and administrators refuse to allow children to stop them from teaching.

• positive supportive attitudes toward children, parents, and education.

3. *Every school needs to be responsive to and encourage parental involvement and input.* That means more than the monthly PTA. It means that parents are not intimidated because they are "only parents," but they are treated as intelligent members of the teaching team. The school should also expect and enlist parental assistance with homework, discipline problems, and supportive attitudes.

As you prepare to tour the schools of your community, clipboard in hand, here are a few specific important things to look at:

• *Classroom arrangement and atmosphere*—Basics schools and most Christian schools usually use some sort of orderly arrangement of desks to encourage a structured type of classroom environment. Some private schools and public schools still use the open classroom arrangement, with little or no structure. Some Christian schools (usually those using the ACE curriculum) place children for the major portion of their day in individual cubicles where they work individually at their own pace.

How do children act in classrooms? Do they seem content, calm, relaxed, happy, or tense, strained, and fearful? Do teachers pay attention to all students or just to a few? How do students and teachers react when a child is in error?

• *Resources and equipment*—Is the library or learning center up-to-date with modern visual aids, clean books, and well-trained, courteous staff? Do children have ample opportunity and encouragement to use the center? Do classrooms have bright, modern maps, clean, fresh bulletin boards, and other attractive learning tools? Is the athletic department stocked with adequate, safe equipment? Does the music department have a good, properly tuned piano and a wide selection of music? Are science labs adequately equipped? Are home economics and industrial arts departments furnished with modern equipment that is kept in good repair? Ancient cooking ranges and treadle sewing machines may do little to attract girls to study home-making arts. This is true especially in our feminist-oriented society.

Many alternative schools operate on shoestring budgets and may be weak in those fringe curriculum areas. Poor equipment is understandable when a school is struggling to get started, but such conditions should be considered temporary. That is especially true of Christian schools. I am reminded of George Mueller who ran several orphanages in nineteenth-century England. Every penny that fed, clothed, housed, and educated those children was a voluntary contribution raised simply through prayer. There was nothing shoddy or second-class about the orphanages. Mr. Mueller believed that "God's work can be done expansively and with quality and we can expect God's supply."[3] Visitors were often amazed at the quality and quantity of facilities and supplies in those homes that were run by faith.

God does not intend that all Christian schools stop charging tuition and seek their funds simply through prayer. Nor should they operate extravagantly. But certainly if Christian education is important, it must be done with an obvious quality that will tell the world that our God is neither sloppy nor poverty-stricken.

• *Philosophy of education*—Not all educators view education from a well-balanced perspective that fits our biblical, whole-person view of education. Do educators perceive that school as a place to provide strong academic education in a positive, strong academic atmosphere, upholding the values of discipline, responsibility, and respect? Do they put undue emphasis on building self-images and development of social skills while letting academics slide? Is their primary goal to manipulate children's value systems and thereby use the school as an agent of social change? Do they fail to provide firm structure for their students, allowing them instead to set their own goals (e.g., deciding what to study and when) and achieve the same through unhindered self-expression? If it is a Christian school, does their goal of religious training seem to be so important that the academic goals are neglected?

Ask to see a school handbook and discover the stated philosophy. Talk with staff members, parents, and teachers to find out what goals the school is pursuing.

• *Rules*—What is expected of students? Of parents? Is there a dress code? If so, is it practical? Is there a schoolwide homework policy? How well are rules enforced? What sort of record does the school have on controlling violence?

• *Faculty/administration relations*—How well does the educational team work together on the campus? Are they in agreement on basic issues such as discipline and academic goals? What is the turnover rate? How do teachers, secretaries, and janitors feel about their principal?

• *Teacher qualifications*—Are teachers certified or credentialed? How long have they been teaching? Are they growing persons, or stagnant pedagogues still teaching identical material in identical ways after twenty years? How do they relate to students?

• *Special education facilities*—If you have children with special needs—either as slow learners or gifted ones—you will want to know what, if any, provision is made for them. Public school systems are required by law to provide special educational facilities for learning disabled children. In many places gifted student programs exist as well. However, many private (both Christian and nonsectarian) and basics schools do not even accept students in any of the several slow learning categories. In addition, they often fail in their highly traditional structure to challenge the bright, gifted children adequately.

• *Problem areas*—Do you have major concerns that the school seems to ignore or not to be able to handle? Can you detect areas of potential conflict between you and the school? Will your child fit in socially? Economically? Academically? Most private schools have rigid entrance standards, including diagnostic tests to determine whether a child can handle the academic challenges of the school. Sometimes they will accept a child who fails the test at his present grade level, provided he is put back one grade. If that happens, you will have to decide which is best—demotion and its possible attendant social trauma, remaining in his present situation, or remaining where he is temporarily while you provide tutoring to bring him up to grade level for another try next year.

Does that Christian or parochial school hold a doctrinal position that you feel you can allow your children to accept? It may be easier to help your child cope with the false teachings of a public system that is obviously not Christian than with the doctrinal differences you may hold with a Christian school.

Is the atmosphere of the Christian school warm and supportive of all Christian students, or are outsiders considered second-class because they wear the wrong denominational tag? I know parents who have taken their children out of parochial schools because of judgmental attitudes displayed there or because the school was used as a soapbox for some pet denominational doctrine.

No school is perfect. Whichever one we choose, we will find problems. We must prayerfully decide which problems we can best live with and still see our children get what we consider to be quality education. One mother told me that her family faced problems with their basics school in one of the classes. "It's still a whole lot better than what we had before," she assured me. "So we will stay with it."

• *Cost*—What sacrifices will you have to make in order to keep your child in that school? One mother had to teach school in order to pay to keep her children in a Christian day school. "But I found myself working fifty hours or more a week and giving my family second best," she admitted. She decided it was not worth that sort of sacrifice.

Many private schools pay their teachers quite poorly. As a result, one of three things may be true: (1) the teachers who work there are exceptionally dedicated to the Lord, (2) they may be such poor teachers that they cannot find higher paying jobs, or (3) the school is plagued with a constant turnover of teachers. Check out those possibilities and determine which, if any, is the case. Again, God's work can afford quality. If we feel that a private education is what our children need, we can trust the Lord to provide the funds so that we can acquire a top quality education.

The single most important question we must ask is this: To whom or what are we actually entrusting the nurturing and keeping of our children's minds and souls? The best school on earth is not trustworthy enough to shoulder such a responsibility. Only God can properly discharge that trust.

Where we send our children to school is vital. It will never be half so crucial as how well we perform our own parental function as their primary educators and how completely we entrust their growth to a loving and capable heavenly Father.

NOTES

1. Dave Raney, "Public School v. Christian School—Which Is Right for Your Child?" *Moody Monthly*, September 1978, p. 46.
2. Jack Layman (headmaster of Ben Lippen School, Asheville, N.C.), "Christian Schools: Pro and Con," *Voices* (Trinity Evangelical Divinity School), Winter 1979.
3. Elizabeth Skoglund, *Coping* (Glendale, Calif.: Gospel Light, Regal, 1979), p. 71.

7

COOPERATING, SUPPLEMENTING, TRUSTING

We should not expect our children to be salt and light there for us, but we should be in there with them to the fullest extent possible, teaching them how.[1]

Jon R. Kennedy

ONCE WE HAVE CHOSEN A SCHOOL for our children, our next challenge is to integrate ourselves into the educational team. That means learning to throw our loyal support behind the school of our choice. Support is not a popular concept today. Criticism is much more fashionable. In fact, if we do not add our voices to the other critics, we are considered naive and undiscriminating. One high school counselor described the climate as follows:

"There is a cold war going on. It is you against us . . . parents versus teachers. This war is fired by the various media, by society and by a changing moral code."[2] Remembering that our battle is not against any school system or staff of educators but against the enemy of our souls, we can approach the teachers of our children with loving attitudes, willing cooperation, efforts to supplement classroom education, and an ultimate trust in God.

What godly attitudes do we need in supporting education? We must begin by being positive. If you were asked to write down all the good things that are happening in American education today, how long would your list be? A negative list would no doubt grow faster and longer. That is because our enemy's first line of attack is against personal confidence in God. Using a kernel of negative truth, he makes sure that we hear predominantly bad reports (often they are exaggerated versions of truth). In that way he makes us problem-

71

centered in our thinking and nourishes the phenomenal growth of fear, worry, and doubt—his favorite weapons for choking out faith.

As my teacher friend Tricia and I lunched at a downtown restaurant one day, we were discussing the improvement of our schools. Suddenly she looked across the street where a major urban redevelopment project was under way. Demolition crews bulldozed through the few remaining relics of the old town.

"That may be the way to rebuild a town," Tricia suggested, "by tearing down the old first and starting over. But when it comes to improving schools, you have to start by building on what's already right."

Now I am asking you to write down all the good things that are happening in your school. Leave plenty of space so you can add to your list in the weeks and months ahead. As you begin your search, you may be surprised at how many constructive features you will uncover. As you continue, you will form the habit of constantly looking for things worth preserving and building on.

When I set out to discover what was right with education today, I found an amazing number of educators and parents eager to share ideas and stories. From Christian day school and basics school leaders, I learned that the fantastic growth in their ranks gives them ample reason to be optimistic about the future of education. I also attended a convention of Christian schoolteachers and administrators, most of whom are in public schools. The mood was unbelievably positive. No one ignored the problems or the frustrations that public school personnel face, but they had stories of God's overcoming power and significant movements in the right direction. One teacher pointed out the changes occurring in attitudes of the general public and courts, toward Christianity and morality in the schools. I came home with a briefcase bulging with documented reasons to rejoice and have great hope.

Being positive about education will lead us to another vital attitude—*respect*. Nothing is more important for a child's educational success than his parents' respect for the school and the authority of its team of educators. Our attitude of respect communicates and reinforces the scriptural principle that "there is no authority except from God and those which exist are established by God. Therefore he who resists authority has opposed the ordinance of God" (Romans 13:1-2, NASB).* Often we need to go out of our way to show our respect

New American Standard Bible.

for teachers by encouraging them as well as righting the wrongs that occur. In the words of one teacher, "The neatest, most uplifting support I've received is Christian parents communicating their support for me by phone calls and notes."

But what about respect when the teacher is teaching things that we as parents do not agree with—things we do not want our children to be taught? That can happen in any kind of school, so we need to be prepared for it. There are several approaches that can help here:

1. Be honest with your child. Admit to him that you know that the teacher is not perfect. Perhaps she is not a Christian and hence does not have a biblical world view. Even as a Christian she is still subject to errors, and we do not do a child any favors by leading him to idolize a Christian teacher to the point of expecting her to be flawless.

2. Encourage your child to obey the teacher, unless she is asking him to do something contrary to God's Word. For example, when taking an exam he may give the teacher the answers she wants. If those answers disagree with the child's convictions, he should write a note to the teacher explaining his own viewpoint. The important thing for the child to learn from this type of encounter is that no teacher's false philosophy negates her God-appointed position of authority.

3. Encourage the child to relate to you the questionable things he hears from the teacher. Do not register shock or jump on the child when he brings home such reports. Instead, react sanely, reminding him of the teacher's humanness. Discuss the idea in the light of scriptural teachings in an attempt to offset whatever negative or false input the child may have received.

4. Tell the child to let you handle the big problems that are too much for him. Come to his aid, but not before he has had a chance to try to work it out for himself. Resist the temptation to side with your child in every conflict. Often children misread what their teachers say and come home with unintentionally distorted reports. Making decisions based on the child's story alone will serve to undermine the teacher's authority. If research proves that there is a problem, discuss it with the teacher, and take it on up through the chain of command in the school if need be.

5. As a last resort, request to have your child moved to another classroom. Some personality problems refuse to be solved. Occasionally you will find a teacher who is incompetent. In such cases, it

is better to change teachers than to allow one teacher to sour a child's attitude toward school or a given subject. Make sure you have done everything possible to salvage a situation before taking such drastic measures.

It helps to remember that no matter how vital the resolution of the immediate problem may be, that is not the most important effect of any student/teacher conflict. The greatest outcome is the instruction such encounters provide in how to handle life's difficulties.

A third attitude essential in supporting education is *enthusiasm.* We show enthusiasm for our children's accomplishments by what we do with their papers when they bring them home, by the questions we ask, the praise we offer, and how faithfully we attend open houses and teacher conferences. One mother calls that the process of nurturing "small accomplishments so larger ones will follow."[3]

The most important way we show our enthusiasm is by being genuinely excited about our own learning process, "even at our age." If I am an enthusiastic, growing adult, the contagion of my attitude will be irresistible. Children rarely need to be cajoled into enjoying learning. The ability to be bored with school is a skill acquired by rubbing shoulders with negative, bored people. A child needs parents and teachers who never let him forget that nothing can be half so exciting as learning.

Finally, we parents owe our children an attitude that says, "*I expect you to learn.*" Children have an intense urge to please both parents and teachers. Our approval is almost literally a life-and-death matter to them. If we are careful to evaluate each child as an individual and set realistically high expectations for him, he will learn. That means taking care to avoid either pressuring the average child to excel beyond his capacities or allowing the genius child to slough off and fail. We communicate these expectations by way of a firm setting of standards and limits, functioning in a warm, supportive, home atmosphere.

Haim Ginott, eminent psychologist specializing in parent/child relations, once stated that "labeling is disabling," and a child frequently lives up to a teacher's negative prediction. He becomes what he is told. If a teacher can wield so much influence by way of expectations communicated to a child, think of the potential power that we as parents hold over them with that simple attitudinal tool.

When our attitudes are right, they will lead naturally to three kinds of supportive actions: (1) cooperating with educators, (2) supplementing classroom education, and (3) trusting the Lord.

Twelve-year-old Michael had changed schools twice in the past school year. In the process, he had received clear messages from some teachers that he was hardly the honor student his elementary teachers had labeled him. So he entered the eight grade with a ho-hum, defeated approach, and did a fantastic job of living up to the low expectations he believed had been set for him.

Michael's mother refused to accept that newly imposed failure image of her son. She visited each of his teachers with an offer of cooperation. Together they discussed the problem and instituted a program whereby Mama would receive weekly progress reports from each teacher. There would be no more excuse for the boy to get behind without knowing it.

"The result was pretty dramatic," says the mother. "Within a few weeks, he went from a D average to an A average. The person it surprised most was Michael."

One junior high counselor told me: "If school and parents can work together, you can make it." Few problems defy solution when parents and teachers learn to cooperate.

Active cooperation begins with detecting problems. One parent commented to me: "So often a problem has become terribly big before I even know it exists. How can I know when problems are developing?"

First of all, we must admit that even our well-trained children from our protected Christian environments are capable of having deep and sometimes even shameful problems. One Christian counselor tells how often teenagers share their problems with her and then add, "If my parents knew I had this problem they would whip me. They are Christians all right, but they just don't think I should have problems, because I am a Christian too."

If we know ourselves and feel secure in the knowledge that our heavenly Father accepts us with all of our own imperfections, we can learn to accept our children in the same way. God is not responsible for our failures. Nor are we totally responsible for the failures of our children.

Beyond that realistic recognition of the potential for trouble, perhaps the most important thing we can do as parents is to keep the channels of communication open between us and our children. Do we really listen to what they are trying to tell us? How much time do we spend with them, giving them our undivided attention? One grandmother who has raised six children suggested that the mother needs to get her household chores out of the way while her child is in school so she can be free to play with him, visit with him, read to him, and so on. For working mothers, that may be impractical. However, we can work together on the chores, sharing in both learning and getting acquainted. The amount of time we spend with our children is not always as important as the quality of that time. Ten minutes of undivided attention may be more effective than a hour of time in the same room when the parent ignores a child's attempts at conversation in favor of the evening paper. We do need to make room in our schedules, however, for the long, leisurely times of family activity. Nothing can substitute for those times.

As we listen, we need to be sensitive to the unspoken messages the child is giving us. We can all learn a lot about body language and the language of behavior. Above all, we must put the child at ease in our presence. If we are continually censoring his words, registering shock at his ideas, stories, or actions, or putting off his questions with unsatisfactory or incomplete answers, we will stop the healthy flow of inner feelings and emotions that he needs to communicate to us.

Make allowances for a child to change with the normal stages of growth. For example, one school principal reminds parents that up to the age of eight, a child is most likely to pay attention when adults speak. Between nine and ten, he will pester other children. After ten, he has an increasing interest in the opposite sex.

Sudden changes in a child's behavior pattern or moods usually signal trouble. When a child loses interest in school or misbehaves, often he is trying to tell the adults in his life that something is amiss. It may indicate some problem with teachers or peers at school. Often educators trace such changes back to a lack of attention at home. The arrival of a new baby, the death of a loved one, a mother going to work, or a divorce may shift the parents' attention from the child to more urgent matters at hand. Lacking the perspective of maturity, he interprets the change as personal rejection and looks for ways to recoup his loss and reinstate his sense of security. Watching for those signals and searching for the reasons behind them is an important part of the parent/teacher cooperation process.

A parent must also ask questions and examine schoolwork. Learn what kinds of testing your child is subjected to and how to interpret his test scores. Discuss them with his teachers and/or counselors (see Resource List for help with this).

Many problems can be detected if you get to know your child's teacher. In the beginning of the year, find out what she expects of your child. Let her know what your expectations are. Make sure you have an understanding that you want to know the instant that any problems begin to show and that you stand ready to do whatever is necessary to work as a part of the team.

If we wait for problems to surface before getting to know the school or the teacher, solution may be considerably more difficult. An excellent rule to follow is to never let ourselves remain strangers to the people who educate our children. To feel that as long as everything is going fine we can let down on our participation in the education process is an attitude that will open the door for untold problems.

Problems or no problems, every parent can cooperate with his child's teachers in dozens of practical ways. We need to regard certain functions as compulsory. *At the least,* parents should attend open houses, concerts, sports events, and parent/teacher conferences (see Appendix 2). Similarly, we must guard against scheduling so many extracurricular activities for our children that their necessary rest and study times are cut short. Teachers have the reasonable right to count on parents to support their demands for homework. One of the foundational principles on which the basics alternative schools are built is the responsibility of parents to see to it that homework is completed on a nightly basis. That means providing for the child a place, a time, and an atmosphere conducive to studying. It means limiting television and/or other distractions. It means sometimes answering his questions and often referring him back to his teacher for further help but never doing the work for him.

We can further cooperate with educators by knowing school policies (dress codes, attendance procedures, discipline, etc.) and enforcing them. We owe it to the child and the school to make sure he eats nutritious foods, gets plenty of rest and exercise, and pays regular visits to the doctor and the dentist.

We can also help our children to develop leadership potential and contribute to the success of their own education. In one junior high school, students, under the direction of a Christian teacher, formed a committee and discovered some effective ways to curb campus violence. The newspaper article that reported the successful venture gave this vital tribute to cooperation from the children's families: "The parents have been supportive and encourage the program."

The second way in which parents must learn to be supportive is in *supplementing classroom instruction.* Such supplementary education may involve using each vacation or family outing as an educational experience. One teacher said he never argues with parents who want to take a child out of school for a short period of time in order to take some educational trip that cannot be done at any other time. (When that gets to be a frequent habit, it is unwise, however.) Educationally guided traveling, in his opinion, is one of the richest sources of education that a child can experience. Sending a child to summer camp can also contribute a great deal.

At times, supplementary education serves a remedial function. A child gets behind for any number of reasons, and we as parents may need to help him catch up. Perhaps the classroom experience is lacking somewhere. We can help here as well. Many children have learned phonics via their mother's instruction and have become far better readers for it.

We supplement a child's education by encouraging his creativity. Every child is born with some degree of creativity, and most children start life with a high degree of it. Most often, the dreary adults who have lost their love affair with life and have got pulled down into the humdrumness of survival, quite adeptly kill that precious commodity. Studies prove that most children's creativity level drops drastically during primary school years. We parents cannot put all the blame on the schools. If we do our part to make sure our children's minds are being constantly challenged and that they receive adequate praise for accomplishments, there is little reason for them to lose the spark of creativity that will allow them to live abundant and fruitful lives.

Finally, our parental-support calling involves an expertise in *trusting God.* No amount of right attitudes or cooperative and supplementary actions will accomplish anything lasting if we do not also apply huge doses of prayer.

We must pray for our children, of course. But how often do we pray for their educators? Prayer can do so much more than criticism, arguments, or legal proceedings. Among all the comments of teachers I have interviewed, the most frequently recurring theme was: "Tell the parents to pray for us." One woman commented: "In our church we pray for the ministers and the missionaries; but I can't remember when, in a prayer meeting, I last heard anybody pray for a school-teacher."

In addition to prayer, we naturally must train our children and do our share of the cooperative work. Beyond that, we can afford to relax and let God shoulder the responsibility for what remains. As we face today's turbulent society, we often find it difficult to maintain that sort of relaxed trust. Personally, I have been greatly encouraged by reading about parents in the dictatorial states of the world. Against the impossible odds of Nazism, Communism, and Fascism, hundreds of godly parents have raised and are raising their children to love the Lord. In oppressed societies, young children are often taken from their homes and retrained in the godless philosophies of their governments. Surely if God can help parents in such circumstances and protect the seed of His Word that has been planted in those children's lives, I can count on Him to do the same for me and my family, whatever may happen in our society in the future. I believe the time has come for us to face the possibility of living with oppression ourselves. If we are to be ready for that day, we must begin now—sharpening the weapons of the heart, learning to trust the Lord with our comparatively small educational problems of today.

"Do not fret," wrote the psalmist, "it leads only to evildoing" (Psalm 37:8, NASB). I have not found one place in my Bible where we are told that because times are dreadfully evil we must sit down and mope about it. Nor that we have a calling to rush around and try to turn other people's confidence into panic. Instead, God instructs us consistently throughout the pages of Scripture to pray, to fight our own battles in His power, to encourage one another, to rejoice, and to believe. "I had fainted, unless I had believed to see the goodness of the LORD in the land of the living" (Psalm 27:13). David's testimony speaks to modern American parents. We too can be saved from fainting on our battlefield only as we lift up our eyes to see what great things God is doing in our educational world and ask Him how we can get involved in the godly action.

NOTES

1. Jon R. Kennedy, "A Not-so-modest Proposal for Reforming American Public Education," *New Reformation,* Christianity on Campus newsletter, Stanford University, March 1979, p. 4.

2. Clyde Wilson, *Jetstream* (parent newsletter of Sunnyvale High School, Sunnyvale, Calif.), editorial, March 1980, p. 1.
3. Donna Foster, "Building Your Child's Self Esteem," *Moody Monthly,* March 1974, p. 98.

8

WHAT ARE OUR RIGHTS?

Children do not belong to the state. They do not belong to us educators, either. They belong to their parents and to nobody else.[1]

Max Rafferty

ONE OF THE FAVORITE PASTIMES of many of the troops assembled at the foot of "Education Hill" is a lively discussion of how public education is falling apart. Among other things, it is fashionable to complain about how students are losing their right to learn, teachers are losing their right to educate, and parents are losing their right to control what goes on in the classroom. All of us read news reports of the threat of total governmental control of education. We hear of a state education code that now reads: "The natural rights of a parent to custody and control of their children are subordinate to the power of the state to provide for the education of children."[2]

We shudder and wail: "Where have our rights gone? What will go next? What hope is left for us?"

In an interview with one high school principal I asked: "What rights do we as parents have left?"

Speaking both as a parent and a school administrator, he answered, "I'm afraid we don't have too many. Increasing bureaucracy, collective bargaining, and the very bigness of education are gradually taking power from the parents."

Basic to all we hear and say is an unquestioning belief that American education at one time embodied a nearly flawless consumer-controlled ideal—a model of excellence for the whole world to emulate. We tend to feel that much of what has happened since *we* graduated from school has contributed to the destruction of that lovely model. One by one we envision our rights being stripped from us by that foreboding "castle on the hill" as it has progressively assumed more power.

In most of our minds, the American education model was housed in the nostalgic atmosphere of a charming, little red schoolhouse. Here some conservative, matronly schoolmarm was hired by the students' parents to stand each day before her well-mannered, knowledge-hungry pupils. With firm discipline and motherly kindness she imparted to them a wealth of information, academic skills, and moral inspiration. The community supported that obviously effective institution and showed its undiluted enthusiasm at spelling bees, Christmas programs, and end-of-the-year picnics.

In actuality, such an idyllic *Saturday Evening Post* cover school is largely a delightful myth. It has erased from our thinking the memory of bullies that chased out unprepared teachers, widespread opposition to the public school concept, rampart trunacy (often parent-supported), high illiteracy rates, and the list goes on. Although this stereotyped concept certainly does not represent the beginnings of American education, it is true that parents, students, and teachers did all enjoy and exercise some rights in the past that we do not have today.

In order to appreciate what rights we have today and learn how to identify, preserve, and use them, we need to look back and see just what happened along the route from the home-centered, community-controlled schools of colonial days to our twentieth-century government-regulated education.

American education was born in the churches and log cabins of early colonial settlements. Agreement on certain Christian values held those infant communities together. One of the most basic of those values was the unquestioned right of the home to educate children. Hence, parents assumed full responsibility for vocational preparation of their children for an early entrance into the work world. The church cooperated with the home in teaching the four Rs, reading, writing, arithmetic, and religion.

With the multicultural development of our nation came many diverse changes and a drastic shift in goals. Man-centered philosophies infiltrated the education system by way of the boarding schools of Europe, where many of the children of wealthy and politically elite colonists got their education. The westward movement placed so much emphasis on the acquisition of land and carving homesteads out of a rugged wilderness that both education and religion slipped down on the priority list. The Industrial Revolution turned people's minds toward material goals. A flood of immigrants, all determined to make it big in America, brought dozens of new value systems into close contact with one another.

In time, America emerged from two world wars with dollar signs in her eyes and a brain filled with dreams of a world perfected by scientific technology. The full scale race began to put an automobile in every garage and a chicken in every pot. The traditional family structure began to break down, as young mothers joined the working force. During a time when parents were almost totally preoccupied with more immediate concerns, John Dewey and other strongly humanistic philosophers began introducing some long overdue changes in the educational system. A new philosophy of parent noninvolvement in education was expressed by John Dewey when he wrote that parents, as untrained nonprofessionals, were a meddlesome hazard to education when they attempted to have a voice in anything more specific than a few "broad policies and ultimate ends affecting the welfare of all."[3]

During the sixties and seventies we passed through the protest-in-search-of-reality challenge to our materialistic ideals. We emerged with a society in which, as one news commentator wrote in 1979, we now have "two cars in every garage and a chicken in every microwave."[4] The feminist movement has flowered into widespread family chaos. Churches are now fighting to save the family from extinction. And the schools? Ah, yes, they are largely influenced by the strong, materialistic goals and the social and economic upheavals of the society that supports them. The real power behind much of their operation is being gobbled up by big government, both state and federal.

But the picture is not totally hopeless for parents. We still have many rights guaranteed to us by the government—rights that most of the rest of the world know little about except in their most idealistic dreams. All we have to do to appreciate that is to read about education and religion in the Soviet Union and the oppression of Christian families behind the Iron Curtain.

Though in their constitutions most Communist countries promise religious freedom, in practice parents are denied the privilege to educate their children according to Christian principles. Fathers are often banished from their families and/or children are taken from parents and placed in institutions as wards of the state. Certainly no educational alternatives are allowed. Mothers must work in factories and usually leave their children, from earliest infancy, in state-operated day-care centers. Older students who insist on living ·by the biblical standards learned from their parents are denied higher education privileges and/or employment and then are often imprisoned for vagrancy.

To those oppressed peoples of the world, our rights would appear incredibly unlimited. However, they are not inalienable. If we fail to properly use and protect them, we could lose them. One man who grew up under Hitler's regime warned: "Freedom is rarely taken away at once. It usually happens slowly and subtly. . . . When Hitler demanded greater and greater sacrifices, resistance became more and more difficult."[5]

An old American saying goes like this: "Eternal vigilance is the price of liberty." How can we maintain that sort of vigilance? We must begin by knowing what rights we have. Unless we know them, we will never be able to protect them.

In America, we enjoy several kinds of rights. We have legal rights of many sorts. There are those rights granted to us by federal laws. They apply to all citizens of the United States. Until recent years, the federally mandated rights of parents and children in education were limited to our constitutional rights of freedom of expression, religion, assembly, and so on. Today, however, the federal government is actively involved in the education process. Laws have been passed to do such things as give parents access to school records, protect the privacy of those records, grant equal opportunity for education of handicapped children, and protect children from psychological testing without parental consent. A host of federally mandated and funded programs now flood our schools, and there are sure to be more to follow. We now have a cabinet level Department of Education to oversee such things.

The bulk of educational laws are state regulations. Rights established by those laws vary from one state to another. For example, the compulsory education laws are state laws and were not all written at the same time.[6] Laws regarding the right to educate your own child at home exist in only thirty-one of the fifty states.[7]

Many rights are protected by all states. It is beyond the scope of this chapter to explain or even list all the rights that may or may not be available to you. In our Resource List you can find a number of

excellent resources to help you discover all your rights. One of those
books summarizes the scope of legal rights universally available as
follows:

> . . . the right to a free education, the right to be protected
> against harm, the right to inspect student records, the right to
> special education for students with special needs, the right to
> due process of law, the right to equal educational opportunity,
> the right of freedom from unreasonable search and seizure, the
> right to freedom of expression and the right to freedom of re-
> ligion and conscience.[8]

Some rights open to parents in all states include the right:

1. To take legal action against a school official in case of "excessive
   or unreasonable" discipline of your child
2. To appeal a suspension of your child
3. To inspect instructional materials used in some federally-funded
   research programs
4. To appeal any school policy that denies a child the right to
   express controversial viewpoints

In addition to federal and state regulations, districts, counties, and
local campuses have their own policies and rules. Some states have
no stated policy on textbook adoption procedures for districts.
Smoking and dress code regulations are usually left to districts and
local campuses. Most parent volunteer programs fall under local and
district jurisdiction.

To learn about local rights, ask your principal or district office.
That information is public record, and we have the right to inspect
and ask questions about it.

The responsible parent will not only learn his present rights, he
will also keep abreast of new and pending legislation that will affect
his rights. We find those things in the news media or in education
newsletters (see Resource List). We can write letters to our legislators
and talk with them when they visit our communities.

Not only do we enjoy legal rights; we have certain human rights as
well. Often, defining those becomes a legal matter, however, especially in present times when basic human values are changing so
rapidly.

As Christians, we have another inalienable right—the right of
access to the God of the universe. His power available to us defies

human imagination. We can expect our God to provide for us all that we need for the whole-person education of our children. That may or may not involve the performance of some miracles such as the removal of an incompetent administrator (consider how much value there is in the removal of an incompetent person if it only means he is passed on to another school), an important change in district policy, or the election of our school board candidate. It may, on the other hand, involve the loss of some legal rights we felt we could not live without. Whatever happens, when we are trusting God and doing our part, we have the absolutely certain right to expect Him to give us only His best.

Knowing the rights, how then shall we use and protect them? Shall we launch a campaign to reinstate prayer and Bible reading in the schools? Shall we demand that our school have a Christmas program? Shall we demand equal time for the teaching of creation along with evolution? Shall we submit meekly to all regulations and allow our children to be subjected to objectionable educational experiments? Shall we try to secure the dismissal of gay teachers? Should we defy the law that refuses to let us educate our children at home? Shall we fight for our students' right to have a Christian club on campus?

As with most problems in education today, there are no simple answers to cover every situation. It helps to realize that those same battles between conflicting philosophical viewpoints are being fought in every arena of society, not just the schools. However, there are six principles that can help us to determine how to answer questions relating to our individual situations and handle our rights in a way that benefits our Christian profession.

First, *a right always carries with it certain responsibilities.* "Christians must see their privileges not as rights to be claimed at all costs, but as opportunities for serving others."[9] Jesus set the example for us when He gave up His rights as God to become a man and procure for us the means of redemption. Rights are granted to protect all persons in a pluralistic society. One of the first things we need to be prepared to do is to give up those personal rights that infringe on the rights of others. The most obnoxious and ungodly way to abuse our rights is to insist on having them regardless of how many other people's rights we destroy in the process.

Bible reading and prayer in the classroom deserve some attention. When the Supreme Court ruled in 1962 and again in 1963 that mandatory prayer and devotional Bible reading were unconstitutional in the public schools, it said in effect, "No child's right to free exercise of religion has the right to infringe on any other child's freedom either to exercise or not to exercise any religion." The judges who handed down that controversial decision also indicated that it would be a great tragedy if the Bible were eliminated from our educational curriculum as a learning tool. School curriculum may legally include a study of Christianity in a course on comparative religions or history. In science classes teachers are free to present creation as an alternative explanation for earth origins. Bible as literature classes are also legal and becoming increasingly popular across the country.*

Second, *before we set out to use a right, we should ask, Why do I feel compelled to insist on the exercise of this right?* Am I trying to prove something or am I trying to protect my child and provide high quality education for him? Will claiming that right help to preserve it for others in the future? In the book *The Christian Teacher and the Law*, Christopher Hall says: "Preoccupation with the exercise of a 'right' rather than preoccupation with the good to be accomplished by the exercise of that right is almost a sure way to overstep the limits of academic freedom granted by the constitution."[10]

A third rule to remember is that *sometimes we must choose the lesser of two evils.* The winning of one rights battle may create other problems of an even more serious nature. Parents can fall quite naively into this trap. A child may be assigned to do something the parents feel violates their convictions as Christians. Immediately, with scarcely a second thought, they rush to the principal and insist that the child be transferred to another class. Certain that they are only demanding their rights, they make such a commotion that the administrator finally grants their wishes. In the new class, however, worse things often befall the child. The teacher may be lax about discipline and requiring students to complete assignments. As a result, the child learns lazy study methods that follow him throughout his education. Meanwhile the parents are so busy rejoicing at the success of their "campaign for righteousness," that they seldom notice what is happening to their child academically in his new situation.

---

*Some Christians fear Bible-as-literature courses because they do not give the Scriptures their due credit as a source of divine revelation. However, when one has studied the Bible as literature, he cannot help seeing that here is a work of literary excellence, unparalleled anywhere else. Just because the teacher does not recognize the power of the Spirit resident on those pages does not keep Him from doing His work in the students' hearts.

Before we claim our rights, we need to ask God to free us from militant attitudes and give us cooperative and supportive ones. When that happens, we will not demand our rights. Rather, we will use and protect them. Demanded rights result in getting what we want by force. Such results can be far from satisfactory. It helps to remember that "a man convinced against his will is of the same opinion still."

The fourth principle is that *we need to become acquainted with the rights of educators as well as our own.* What rights does our child's teacher have? If we know them, then we can set reasonable expectations of her. Does she know her legal boundaries? Probably not too many of them. As a consequence, she may be acting out of intimidation by superiors who are no more familiar with them than she is. We can help there as well. One teacher suggested that parents should present books on teacher and parent rights to their teachers and/or administrators (see Resource List).

We can also actively support the rights of a teacher and/or administrator. At times that means coming to his or her rescue when some of those important rights are being threatened.

A fifth principle is that *God has admonished us to "submit [our]-selves to every ordinance of man"* (1 Peter 2:13, italics added). Only when God's laws conflict with man's are we free from that obligation. Even then we must proceed with caution and a right spirit. In every place where the New Testament writers mention the relationship between the church and government, they always urge us to pray—never to rebel or protest. That scriptural principle applies to us today as well as to the first-century believers. The only difference is that we have recourse, in America, to the democratic process. As long as the avenue of legal change is open to us, we must use it.

Finally, we must exercise the *right to ask the schools to live up to their stated goals.* If a school states that its aim is to educate students in the basic skills, then parents have the right and duty to hold the educational team of that school accountable for training their children in basic skills. Some parents are taking advantage of that right today by suing school districts when their students fail to graduate from high school because they cannot pass minimum competency tests. That kind of action is faulty, because it does not accomplish the thing we parents most want to see done. The most it can do is to alert the educational system that parents expect better quality teaching. However, large sums of money will never compensate for a lost education.

The time to find out whether a child is learning basic skills and do something about it is not at the end of high school but in grade one, while the problem can still be corrected.

Regardless of the ugly rumors we hear among the battle troops where we have enlisted, we can rest assured that we do still have all the rights we need to allow us to provide a quality education for our children. Even if we have to resort to the right to seek an alternative education, the goal can be achieved. If we are to win the big war and not just today's skirmish, we must learn when to claim those rights and when to find other means of dealing with the problems that challenge our creative battling.

NOTES

1. Max Rafferty, *Max Rafferty on Education* (New York: Devin-Adair, 1968), p. 9.
2. Revised Education Code, Ohio School Guide Sect. 7.06, Compulsory Education Law, p. 195.
3. John Dewey, *Moral Principles in Education* (New York: Philosophical Library, 1959), pp. vi-vii.
4. *San Jose Mercury*, editorial, 4 July 1979.
5. Helmut Ziefle, "A Christian Family Resists Hitler," *Christianity Today*, 15 December 1978, p. 24.
6. *Information Please Almanac, 1980*, p. 737.
7. *Parent Rights Card*, Columbia, Maryland, National Committee for Citizens in Education (NCCE).
8. David Schimmel and Louis Fischer, *The Rights of Parents in the Education of Their Children* (Columbia, Maryland: NCCE, 1977), p. 1.
9. Leon Morris, "The Responsible Make Legends Happen," *Christianity Today*, 7 September 1979, p. 78.
10. Christopher Hall, *The Christian Teacher and the Law* (Oak Park, Ill.: Christian Legal Society, 1975), p. 33.

9

GETTING ACTION

The world is looking for quick-fix solutions to chronic problems and this is dangerous.[1]

A. Graham Down

MR. S_____'S DAUGHTER brought home complaints that her teacher was using profanity in the classroom. The father went immediately to the teacher and requested that such carryings on cease. The teacher responded promptly, and the offended daughter never again heard foul language in her class.

An Ohio mother was found guilty of violating truancy laws when she sent her daughter to an unchartered Christian school. She appealed the court decision, and her conviction was reversed. (This account was taken from *Eternity*, February 1978, p. 11.)

When a county schools superintendent announced that a teacher's workshop would be held on a controversial sex education guide, a spokesman for a group of parents informed him that between three and four hundred parents planned to protest at a county board of education meeting. The superintendent canceled the workshop. (*San Jose Mercury*, 16 April 1980.)

A group of students in southern California took their district to court, suing them for banning their campus Bible study—a breach of agreement between students and district trustees. (*Moody Monthly*, April 1976, p. 11.)

Those parents and students illustrate for us a variety of possible means for facing the problems in education. Regardless of what school we have chosen, we will face issues that demand some sort of involved action. As with everything else in life, there are always objectionable ways to tackle a problem as well as effective ones.

Nancy Larrick, in her book *A Parent's Guide To Children's Educa-*

tion, summarizes the objectionable battle tactics of persons whom she calls "dedicated souls who are dedicated to the wrong things," under these headings:

1. Self-appointed censors, who feel it is their duty to discover and expose all the incriminating evidence.
2. People whose philosophy is "Let's make it tough on the educators. Never let them forget that we are here, dogging their every step."
3. Those whose call is, "Let's go back to the good old days and do it the way my teachers did it." (This sounds a bit like the "when-I-was-a-girl" approach to parenthood, and it works about as well.)
4. Penny pinchers unlimited—responsible, thrifty souls who are "against anything that costs money, regardless of the need."[2]

We might add to this list a fifth category—those idealistic, non-involvement types who believe that if they ignore the problem, it will surely go away or prove itself not to be such a big thing after all.

We live in times when much prayer is desperately needed. Action without prayer can be dangerous indeed. At the same time, "prayer can be dangerous whenever it becomes a substitute for action."[3] Actually, prayer often helps us to know what action we must take.

Education is a vital functioning part of our society. As one district administrator told me: "Public education happens under a magnifying glass. It's a matter of people taking time and having the courage to fight for what they feel is right." Then he added, "One of the major objectives of public officials is to be responsive to our constituency. . . . *We want you to react.*"

If our educators have failed to meet our expectations, is it possible that we have never bothered to tell them what we want? Have we taken for granted that we all want the same things?

One way to make our wishes known and get action is by electing to all levels of public office persons with a strong, sensible philosophy of and commitment to education. In chapter 13 we shall list some of the things to look for in a candidate for public office. We need also to closely examine ballot measures to see what the implications are for education. A petition was circulating in our state to place on our ballots a measure that would eliminate the state inheritance tax. One woman in our community told an audience of school parents that she had decided to read the fine print. Here she found that a substantial portion of the inheritance tax money goes for the funding of education. Having felt the pinch of other good-sounding fiscal propositions that have occasioned the death of school programs, she reconsidered and finally did not sign the petition.

The most important way for parents to become actively involved is to speak up. How do we do that?

Several years ago, I was given a petition to sign. It urged educational authorities to bring their programs into line with a list of godly expectations and goals. Everything on the petition represented my own philosophy of an ideal education. But when I showed it to a teacher friend, her reaction was quick: "Petitions of that kind are an escape technique. It is so easy to sign them without actually knowing what is going on and then go on our way without getting constructively involved."

I thought a lot about what she said. I never signed the petition. Instead, I redoubled my efforts to learn all I could about what was happening and to offer my services in every place possible.

Petitions do have their place. Many have saved teachers' jobs, gotten rid of objectionable textbooks, and rescued threatened school programs, but a far more influential way to speak up is by letter, telegram, or mailgram. Public servants are much more impressed by a letter which gives evidence that we understand the problem, have thought the issue through for ourselves, and have sane reasons for our feelings, than by thousands of signatures on a petition or duplicate letters (see Appendix 6).

When you send a letter to a local school board, address it to both the district superintendent and the school board. Send copies as well to the school principal, teachers, legislators—all the people who are involved or should know about your concern. Write letters to the editors of local newspapers. The editorial section is one of the most read sections of the paper, and it is an excellent forum for influencing public opinion. Take advantage also of television and radio talk shows and free speech messages. The mass media belongs to the people in our democratic society. If we abdicate our rights to use those tools to the spokesmen for evil causes, we have no one but ourselves to blame when public opinion does not go the way we would like to see it go. We may not move the masses by those campaigns, but at least we allow our ideals to get an exposure. Who knows how many people we may challenge to a new way of thinking?

There is also a time for "eyeballing" or telephoning the educator or public official. In-person conferences are generally preferable to telephone calls. One counselor says that he believes that parents show more genuine concern if both parents come in for a conference. Attending school board meetings is an excellent way to ask questions, get information, or express an opinion. Regular attendance at those meetings is one of the best possible methods of getting acquainted with board members and the goals, attitudes, and value systems of your school district.

Another effective method for speaking up is to join a school-site council or advisory committee. The popularity of those committees has grown in the past few years. I have personally served in such capacities and have seen many of my ideas not only listened to but put into action as well.

At times our cause is of such magnitude that we need to form a group of like-minded parents and work out our problem together (see Appendix 5). Many organizations do a lot of work in dozens of areas of education today. A group may simply be a local assembly of parents who protest some immediate issue. One such group formed to object to a sex education plan in New York State. They recruited sympathetic parents with an explanatory flier distributed throughout the city. Then they organized, presented their cause to the school board, got what they wanted, and disbanded. "If we need to re-form, we can do it again," said the leader.

Other groups are formed to meet a need for continuing action. One such committee in Canada exerts pressure on schools to secure a variety of improvements in education. Another group in Arizona started small when one parent saw something she did not like and decided to find out what was going on. The group grew into a local organization that researched issues and informed parents. Today they publish their findings in a letter that is circulated in most of the states and a few foreign countries.

A group in Ohio serves a more activistic function. They too publish a newsletter with nationwide circulation, but they often draw up statements of their specific concerns and take them to their state legislature. They make up a small lobby group in their state capital.

One other area of growing concern for parental involvement is that of collective bargaining and teacher strikes. Parents can play a key role in the settling of those disputes. Our children are the ones being manipulated, and elected officials are sensitive to the wishes of the community that elects them. Before we get involved here, we need to understand the collective bargaining process and know how to do our part effectively without having to resort to terrorist methods such as harrassing school board members and storming the doors of the "castle on the hill." In the Resource List, I have mentioned sources for some helpful booklets to give you know-how and guidance for your involvement in such disputes.

How we get involved and what we do depends upon many things. As we immerse ourselves in the situation and pray for constant wisdom, we will find our place. Before we rush off to battle, let us stop and look at five guidelines to guard against wasted efforts and harmful head-lopping.

First, *we need to be informed*—to find out our position and that of our educators. Are we in agreement with the powers that be? Is the atmosphere conducive to teamwork, or will we have to help create that sort of climate?

Always get the facts before taking any action. Verify what you read. Read all you can on every side of a controversial issue. Be suspicious of reports of extreme circumstances or suggested extreme solutions. We cannot afford to let it be said of us as Paul said of the Jews of his day: "To their zeal for God I can testify; but it is an ill-informed zeal" (Romans 10:2, NEB).*

Some schools and districts have founded a system known as "Key Communicators" to provide a helpful solution to the problem of destructive rumors. Perhaps the Lord would give you a ministry of setting up such a system for your school or your district (see Appendix 4 for instructions).

Another part of being informed is knowing all the people involved in the education process. Do we know our children? If not, how can we presume to know how they ought to be dealt with? One father was urged by school authorities to get psychiatric help for his adopted son.

"He doesn't need counseling," the father told administrators. "He simply needs some solid, structural expectations. Demand performance from him, and his problems will be solved." The principal and teacher followed the father's advice and soon they admitted: "You were right. Your son's problem was really a need for more discipline."

Do we know ourselves? We must ask: Am I the leader type who can run the PTA? Would I function better as a classroom aide or campaign manager for some school board candidate? Maybe I can stuff envelopes for a school organization or help students in the

New English Bible.

library. We need to know our own limitations in order to act responsibly.

Do we know where the power is in our school structure? Some schools are most influenced by local school boards. In other areas, the greatest power lies with the principal. In still others, the state is the big power-wielder. Find out where the power is in your situation. It may be difficult. Ask questions, test cases, look at budgets, get involved at every level possible, and observe who has the last word on issues. That will give you a clue as to the seat of power. Learn procedures for presenting your cause to the district or state. Know the rules and abide by them.

Do we know what goes on in our children's schools? Open houses, programs, parent-teacher conferences, and visits to the library, the classroom, the cafeteria, and the playground are available. How many do we take advantage of? (It is imperative that you register in your school office before visiting a school campus during school hours. Persons who simply wander onto school grounds are usually suspect of malicious motives.) Are we total strangers in our children's world?

Second, *we must be positive.* The positive approach wins friends and support. Negativism antagonizes the very persons we need to help us. I think we are rarely aware of how much destructive poison we spread or how much damage we inflict on our children when we spew disgruntled gripes in every direction within their earshot instead of going to the proper authorities and seeking sane solutions.

How often do we send a note to a teacher thanking her for what she has done to help our child? I remember hearing a principal once say: "I receive very few thank-yous but a lot of nasty complaints." How about writing to the principal or the school board with a word of commendation for some teacher, janitor, or other person on the school team? One of the teachers who taught all three of my children received quite a few thank-yous from me over the years. She now tells me: "One positive note can provide energy for low days and can revitalize even an assumed negative person. I have every one of your beautiful handwritten notes in my 'personal warm fuzzy file'—eight years' worth!"

Being positive also means offering constructive ideas. Alistair Cooke once noted that "men who love the bonfire find the rebuilding a bore." Let us ask God to give us a rebuilder's heart.

Third, *we must learn to be courteous.* Rudeness and accusations that spread like wildfire rarely accomplish anything more than to arouse bad feelings. A shouting activist would do more good if he stayed at home behind locked doors and shuttered windows and never got involved. James had a word about that: "But let every one be quick to hear, slow to speak and slow to anger; for the anger of man does not achieve the righteousness of God" (James 1:19-20, NASB). When I treat a school official, teacher, or janitor rudely, I am telling him: "I do not care a fig about you." Frankly, I find it hard to believe that God wants me to do His work in this way.

To be courteous means to go to the right person at the right time with my problem. Start with the person closest to the source of the problem. If I have a complaint against a teacher, the courteous thing to do is to go to the teacher first. If I get no satisfactory action, then I may have to go to the principal and on up the line as far as it is necessary. I must get to know the chain of command in my system and use it.

Courtesy also involves being calm. "Don't storm the Bastille!" warned one parent who had learned the secrets of getting action. "If you are angry, cool off first. Go and let them know that you need help, that you feel they have answers, and that you will be happy to cooperate with them in solving this problem."

"I always try to attack the problem, not the individual," writes one teacher.

If we are courteous, we will be specific in our complaints and/or requests. For example, when I say to a teacher, "My son simply isn't doing well," that leaves her wondering what I mean and how to translate my complaint into action. But if I say, "My son is not learning to read. I think he is having trouble with certain letters," then we have something to work with. The general vague comment forms a negative attack against the teacher's abilities to teach. The specific statement gives evidence that the parent is requesting help for something very definite, confined to one area.

Finally, courtesy involves sticking to the issues and not trying to make the school system or some educator look bad. When I resort to ridicule of the other person, then I stoop to a level that is unworthy of my Christian testimony. I also close the doors for future cooperative efforts. A group of Maryland parents obtained a change in school board policy for their learning disability children. They accepted the change with gratitude, saying: "We didn't ask for a letter from the school system, saying 'We were wrong.' The less hoopla the better.

. . . This kind of publicity only increases the anxiety level of school officials the next time we approach them."⁴

Fourth, *we need to be confident.* Panicky people do not use their heads. They do not trust the Lord, and they do not take responsibility for their actions. When we have set our goals, prepared our children, chosen the right schools and done all that reason, courtesy, and God's wisdom direct in collaboration with the God of the universe, we can afford to be confident of our actions and the outcome.

In one instance, another parent and her daughter and I found ourselves in a conference opposing the principal, a drama teacher with her lawyer, and the English department head. Our purpose was to stop the production of a certain play. I had had several previous sessions with the teacher and the vice-principal. Now I was there to support the student in her efforts. We laid out our objections and talked it over as sanely as possible. At the end of the conference, we were told that the play would go on. The other mother and I could do nothing more except trust God to guide our daughters in choosing between right and wrong.

Finally, if we are to get action, *we need to be persistent.* Many of us possess an amazing ability to begin projects well. But enthusiasm peters out quickly when we begin to suspect that our opponents know more than we do. If you as a parent are like I am, you have a natural tendency to shrink in the presence of a professional educator. Looking back over my involvement record, I see a number of aborted ventures when I lacked either the time, the self-confidence, or the determination to carry through to completion.

I have learned that it pays to count the cost before approaching any battlefield. No battle yields to the undisciplined, recalcitrant soldier. Furthermore, battles we win today may be lost tomorrow if we do not exercise continued vigilance to protect our victories from fresh attacks.

It occurs to me that among the ranks of concerned Christian parents in America today, lies an almost unlimited potential to get all the action we need. If we would just ask God to release us from our fears, cleanse us from our negative attitudes, and then set ourselves to band together and carry through with everything we begin, who can predict the results? Whatever we do, we bequeath the results to our children and grandchildren; that should be worth all the effort.

NOTES

1. *Basic Education* (news clipping, "David and Goliath"), November 1979, p. 8.
2. Nancy Larrick, *A Parent's Guide to Children's Education* (New York: Trident, 1963), pp. 374-76.
3. Charles Sell, "How to Faith It," *Moody Monthly*, March 1978, p. 40.
4. *NETWORK* (NCCE newspaper for parents), March 1979, p. 2.

10

WHO PAYS THE BILLS AND HOW?

*Well informed citizens can . . . help channel more school
dollars into programs that help children most . . . regardless
of enrollment trends.*[1]

NCCE

EDUCATION COSTS MONEY—lots of money! To educate one pupil for a
school year in 1978-79 cost between $1,200 in Arkansas and $3,900 in
Alaska. During the past ten years, public education costs have "increased 187 percent, more than twice the rate of other consumer
goods and services."[2]

Who pays those monstrous bills? Who decides how much money
is needed and for what? Do parents have the right to know details
about school budgets—to have a voice in planning them?

Those are important questions we need to answer as we prepare to
go into action. The answer to the first question is painfully obvious.
You and I, the taxpayers, pay the bills for public education. How do
we pay? Through local taxes? Federal taxes? State taxes? How does
the money get from our paychecks to the school down the block?

School financing presents one huge and confusing picture. The
situation varies widely from state to state and never stays the same.
New legislation, voter initiatives, increased involvement of the federal
government, plans to revamp the whole school financing structure—
all those keep things changing so fast that even educators have to
read the morning newspapers to learn the prospective fate of their
special projects and their jobs.

Any time we have questions about local school or district budgets,
we should never hesitate to go to the principal or the district superintendent's office. Districts usually have one person in charge of

budgetary matters. School board and budget committee members can also answer questions. Write your state legislators for state budgetary questions.

But first, a few facts and general policies will give us some background and help us begin to unscramble the whole disarrayed picture and interpret the current trends.

Schools receive their funding from three basic sources: federal, state, and local tax monies. The first of those sources—federal taxes—is a relatively recent one. In fact, at the beginning of the nineteenth century the American school system did not exist, and the US Constitution did not even mention education. According to the Bill of Rights, "the powers not delegated to the United States by the Constitution, nor prohibited by it to the States, are reserved to the States respectively, or to the people."

Consequently, education became the function of state and local governments. Not until Congress passed and funded the National Defense Education Act in 1958 did the federal government get involved in financing public education. Since then, our federal legislators have passed a number of bills to appropriate funds for many things—school lunch programs, vocational education, handicapped education, minority opportunity funds, emergency funds, and curriculum research grants.

As we near the end of another century, not only does Washington have a cabinet level Department of Education, but also our federal government exerts strong pressure on school districts by way of a growing number of federally funded educational assistance programs. Those programs total somewhere between 7 and 10 percent of our education income in a given year. The pressure is often great, because with each program comes a list of regulations. The burgeoning mountain of paperwork involved is enough to irritate and discourage the neediest administrator.

Several years ago, I had a firsthand experience with federal string-attachment. Our school-site council was helping the district review proposed budget cuts in the wake of the California state property tax limitation initiative—Proposition 13. Among other things, we examined our expensive lunch program. Our school serves a high percentage of minority and low-income students and must foot quite a high bill for free lunches. Students and staff members on the council observed that many of the needy students were either selling their free tickets or depositing their lunches in the nearest trash can. So, we asked if an outside source could be contracted to provide inexpensive bag lunches that would probably be more readily accepted by the students. The answer came wrapped in federal red tape. Our free lunch program was federally mandated on a matching fund basis. As such, the menu was subject to federal regulation and cold sandwiches did not meet the requirements.

State education departments fund an increasingly large percentage of the education bill. One set of figures showed that the average state aid had increased from 39 percent to 44 percent in the past ten years.[3] Even though property taxes have in the past provided as much as 98 percent of a school's budget, they have not always been strictly local taxes, in that their expenditure has been largely controlled by the state. Today most states tell us how much we can collect, how we can use it, and even how much of it we must give to other districts.

In 1977, for example, the California legislature passed a bill that represented a long-time popular trend in educational thinking. Other states have followed that trend as well. According to the current legislation, a wealthy school district cannot spend any more local property tax money per student than a poorer district. All monies are channeled through and apportioned out equally by the state.

Just as the bill was going into effect, the citizens of our state passed Proposition 13. Though the proposition was aimed at cutting state spending, it attacked local property tax levels. The result? Schools became even more dependent on our state department of education not only for funds, but for a host of new regulations telling us how we may spend what money.

Local property taxes are less and less reliable as a source of income. In states where they are still used to finance education, such taxes must be voted on by local citizens. And the success record of education bond issues has declined sharply in recent years. I have knocked on doors seeking support of school bonds, and I know the kinds of reservations people have. Older persons living on fixed incomes are naturally more concerned about making their meager pension resources stretch in today's inflationary society than sacrificing for schools to spend their money in ways that they know they cannot monitor and that are perhaps ineffective. The situation is not going to improve in the near future, with the decreasing birth rate and rise in average age of Americans. Parents often feel that schools are wasteful and need to learn to trim the fat as the rest of us are doing at home. One couple told me that they refused to go on raising their own taxes and then watch the increase disappear into the common pot to support poorer districts. There are also the hundreds of thousands now paying double for education—taxes plus private school tuition.

Parochial and private schools do not depend on government funding sources. Parochial schools receive funds from their denominational organizations and private contributions in addition to tuitions. Independent private and Christian day schools depend almost entirely on tuition fees, contributions, and foundation grants. Some of the private schools in all those categories receive some public assistance in the form of such things as transportation, textbooks, shared school facilities (libraries, athletic fields, and so on).

It should be noted that most of the basic education alternative schools refuse assistance from all but mandatory federal programs. They prefer seeking other sources of income with "no strings attached." Being a part of the public school system, they do not charge tuition fees. Many of them receive partial assistance, however, from private donations and/or foundational grants.

In addition to the more or less predictable income sources, all kinds of schools launch a variety of fund-raising projects. Carnivals, bake sales, student walkathons, paper drives, and candy or miscellaneous sales are popular methods for raising extra money either for special needs or, in the case of the private or basics schools, general expenses.

Once the money is provided, who decides how it will be spent? Who plans the school budget? Every department of education, from the federal Department of Education on down the line, has its own budget. Further, both federal and state boards of education pass on to local districts a growing number of regulations regarding the allocation of funds. But when it comes to the neighborhood campus, specific budget planning begins with the district school board or board of trustees. In many states, the district budget becomes an item for collective bargaining between teachers and administrators. Procedures vary from state to state and district to district, but generally a school principal is responsible to plan for specific expenditures on his campus within the framework constructed for him by the district.

Where do the parents come into the picture? Do we have the right to know details about school budgets? Can we have a voice in planning them? The title of one book for parents gives a clear answer: *The School Budget: It's Your Money—It's Your Business.* When our representatives, the school board officials, sit down to decide how they will spend our tax monies, yes, we do have the right to know the details. Parents in schools with certain kinds of specific programs funds, known as categorical funding, are required to be invited to serve on advisory committees to approve at least parts of the budget.

Many parents do not have the slightest idea where to begin in the budgetary process. Nor should all parents attempt to enter the front lines of the battlefield. School budgets are complicated, and for the most part we do not understand what is going on. I know. I have attended public hearings of our school board for the discussion of budget proposals. I confess that those hearings left me quite confused.

I learned a bit about what makes a school budget work as I served on our school-site council. Rhoda Dersch, author of *The School Budget: It's Your Money—It's Your Business,* claims she learned about budgets by studying them and getting involved one step at a time. She points out that school budgets can be "demystified" by any citizen who has "a willingness to work, a pocket calculator and the conviction that the school budget is your business."[4]

Today, when our whole citizenry is keenly aware of the need for public officials to be accountable to us as to how they spend our tax money, many people are doing their research and speaking up. In one issue of an education newspaper, I read about parent groups in South Carolina, Minnesota, New York, Michigan, Maryland, and Rhode Island who are investigating budget processes, assessing situations, and making recommendations to their school boards for changes in the budgetary structure.[5] At this point, they have not yet had sufficient time to prove how effective they can be. The whole idea of parent-citizen groups lobbying school board budgetary processes is a new thing. In a day when citizens are demanding a hearing and educators are begging for community input, the time seems to be ripe for such action.

Most school boards have budget committees. That is an excellent place for parents to begin learning. The current president of our elementary school district got her start in school politics by serving on the budget committee.

We parents need to be realistic as we face budget matters. We must begin by remembering the limitations imposed on our boards of education by both federal and state hierarchies. Obviously, we should not attempt to defend the programs that affect our children at the expense of some other programs that may be important to a greater number of students. At times, it is hard to see those issues from objective viewpoints, but we must ask God to give us clear vision. When some elective program succumbs to the slash of a budget knife, perhaps we should take that as a clue to search for creative ways to provide the same services through community volunteer programs. That is an excellent opportunity for churches to serve community needs. Some are doing it already. I think we will see a great deal more of that in coming years as cuts increase all across the country (see chapter 12 on ideas for volunteer programs).

Working to adjust inequities and eliminate waste in education budgets demands the application of a lot of common sense and creative alternative planning. In Appendix 7 you will find a list of nineteen ways to check the rising cost of education without cutting quality. Study the list; let it launch you on an exciting, creative, budget-trimming campaign to serve your school.

In response to the difficult, crisis-proportioned problems of modern education, several radical solutions are being widely discussed and attempted. We need to look at a couple of those. If you have not already met with them, you undoubtedly will before you are through educating your family. You will probably be called on to support or vote on some of those issues.

The first has to do with government aid to private schools. It would be provided either in the form of direct grants to the schools or by tax breaks for parents who are paying private school tuition fees. For years, parents who have educated their children outside the public system have had to pay double—once through taxes and again through tuition bills. "We see no reason why we should pay for the public schools, then turn around and pay tuition to make sure that our children get an adequate education," one couple told me.

Many people feel that the government owes it to its citizens to grant some form of aid to church-related schools. "It is astonishing that the government pays for the education of children in public schools, but not for the education of children in independent schools,"[6] wrote a pastor.

Proponents of this idea feel that such a move would improve the quality of education for all—for private schools by giving them greater resources and for the public schools by providing them with healthy competition. Above all, they believe that it is hardly fair for tax monies to be used to support what the federal government has ruled is a religion—secular humanism—while refusing to support schools that teach traditional religious ideals.

Although that idea has been batted around for a very long time and has surfaced in the legislature many times, it seems to be more feared than trusted. Legislators see it as a dangerous excursion into the area of state intervention in church affairs. Many church schools have stated that they would reject such funds. As we have already observed, federal funds never come without regulations and those proverbial "strings." In government, as in any other area of life, he who holds the purse makes the rules. Church schools today encounter enough hassles with the government over regulation of curriculum, textbooks, and education standards. Receiving government funds would only escalate the process and eventually make alternative education a myth hidden behind church doors.

A second suggestion is closely related but much more alive and well today. In fact, once someone perfects the plan to make it sufficiently plausible to satisfy a wide enough variety of people, you and I will no doubt be called upon to vote on it in our states within the next few years. I refer to the *voucher system.*

Dozens of different voucher plans have been proposed, each with its own variations. Basically, all parents would be given government-funded coupons for the financing of their children's education. Those coupons would be redeemable at the school (public or private) of their choice. In most cases, transportation would be provided for all at public expense.

Sounds great, does it not? I have talked to parents and teachers who think that it is the ideal solution to the largest number of our problems. Most of their thinking sounds like the statement of Robert Love in his book *How to Start Your Own School:* "The one sure way we can improve education in America is by making the educational system competitive, with parents and students able to do 'comparison shopping.' "[7] Certainly the use of vouchers would provide a strong element of competition.

Parents would also be able to choose for their children without having to consider whether they could afford it. Many point to that as a much purer form of free education for all than can ever be possible under our present system. It would provide a more voluntary method for integrating students. No longer would the private school be restricted simply to the wealthy child. Classes would be allowed to mix in the alternative schools in much the same way that they do in public schools today.

Still there are problems. If the system is put into operation at a totally unrestricted level, we might soon see an unprecedented growth of small schools. "I would start my own school," one high school counselor told me. If he would, we all know of a dozen others who would follow suit. Before long, education in such a climate would develop a patchwork personality with little continuity and a tendency to instability.

On the other hand, if too many restrictions are placed on voucher schools, then the alternatives lose their freedom to maintain the distinctive features that were their reason for coming into being. Many people fear that under the voucher system public schools would continue to function largely for those whose parents cannot be bothered to shop around—the type of parents that never attend open houses under our present system. It is not difficult to imagine what sort of schools they would become under those circumstances. Others believe that once more the wealthy who can afford to pad their government coupons from their own pockets would do so and form yet another exclusive class of schools. Sound familiar?

In the final analysis, I think it is fair to ask whether the voucher system is really just the federal-aid-to-private-education solution, all spruced up with a new feather in its old felt hat (see Appendix 8).

When it comes time to cast our votes on those things, we need to examine all the angles, read the fine print, decipher all the implications, and pray a lot before we go to the polls.

Many of us would like to push back the calendar a few decades so we could simplify educational financing and regain control of the educational purses without a struggle. We know that is unrealistic, but visiting budget offices, learning all we can, offering our services, subtle hints, and strong suggestions are very realistic indeed. If in the process we find ourselves faced with a duel we must fight, then we can polish up our armor—spiritual and intellectual—and take on the toughest challenge for the glory of God and the education of our children.

NOTES

1. From report on school financing in *NETWORK*, April 1979, p. 3.
2. "Higher Cost, Lower Enrollment," *NETWORK*, March 1979, p. 4.
3. Ibid.
4. Rhoda E. Dersh, *The School Budget: It's Your Money—It's Your Business*, Columbia, Maryland: NCCE, 1979, pp. 3-4.
5. *NETWORK*, April 1979, pp. 2-3.
6. Edwin H. Palmer, "Should the Government Support Church-Related Schools?" *Eternity*, May 1972, p. 12.
7. Robert Love, *How to Start Your Own School* (Ottawa, Ill.: Green Hill Publ., 1973), p. 3.

11

THE TEXTBOOK ARENA

The textbook battle is . . . a necessary effort of ordinary families determined to preserve and live their Christian way of life.[1]

John B. Conlan

"Mother Protests Use of Evolution Textbook"—the newspaper head-line grabbed Nancy's eyes as she scanned the page of local stories. Nancy and her husband had several children in the public schools. Perhaps they too were being taught from such textbooks. During the next weeks she followed the pictures and stories of the campaign of a woman who was disturbed enough over one objectionable book to make a lot of noise about it. Nancy rejoiced when finally the woman succeeded in removing the book from both the library and class-rooms of her school.

"If that woman can take a stand, so can I," Nancy told herself. She began praying and looking for someone to lead a movement in the schools of her area, to make it possible for public school students to hear the scientific evidences of creation in their classrooms. The Lord answered first by leading her to several people who were already doing that sort of thing in other areas. Two mothers were actually carrying their campaign to the state capitol. Still no leader emerged on her local horizon.

Then one day Nancy's daughter heard a convincing classroom pre-sentation of the evolution of the horse. She rushed home to tell her mother and asked, "Mom, how do we know the Bible is true? Evolu-tion is in my science book. It must be true!"

Promptly the mother went to her daughter's teacher and expressed her concern. "I never intended to destroy any child's faith," the teacher responded. She was open to Nancy's concern and did what she could to correct the situation created by an unquestioning use of a textbook.

At this point Nancy began to realize that the Lord had been grooming and nudging her to become the leader of the new movement she had been praying for. Seeking guidance from her friends active in other areas, she decided not to ask for the elimination of evolution from the currciula. Rather, she sought district approval for a policy that would allow and encourage teachers to present creation, as well as evolution, as a viable, scientific explanation of origins.

She started with her own school library where she discovered an appalling imbalance of evolution and creation materials. She reported her findings to the principal, who invited her to share them with the Home and School Club. Parents were impressed, some even angry; but when it came to action, they were not ready to move. Nancy began to wonder about the whole project, but the Lord showed her that it was His project, and He wanted her to push on.

She began talking with people everywhere she went about creation and evolution in education. In that way, she gathered around her a group of parents who were already involved as leaders in their own schools and were known and accepted in the district office as members of the education team. Together they called on the district superintendent, whom they found to be sympathetic to their wishes.

Later, when opposition arose in a nearby district, they took a survey of community opinion. That survey revealed that an overwhelming majority of the citizens favored their cause, including 75 percent of the evolutionists questioned. They wrote letters to newspaper editors, called talk shows, and recorded free speech message spots on both radio and television. Finally, after several months of intensive work, they won a monumental victory. The school board issued a directive that adjusted district policy to encourage a fair presentation of creation along with evolution in the classrooms of the district. The district superintendent further supported Nancy's and her friends' new ventures—public education meetings for training teachers in the scientific bases of creationism and debates and lectures by respected authorities.

Seven years after she first read that newspaper article, Nancy now heads an organization called Citizens for Scientific Creation. They continue to train teachers and sponsor debates and lectures, as well as to provide a bank of experts who can lecture on creationism in classrooms, and to offer education to parents on how to deal with the issue in their own situations. She has served on the textbook adoption committee for her state.

Nancy's success story illustrates the fact that many parents in our society are concerned to the extent of doing something about the kinds of textbooks and supplementary books that our children are using in their classrooms and learning centers. Their concern is not unfounded. In one survey done in 1976, it was determined that next to the teacher, the single most important element in influencing the classroom education of children was the textbook.[2] The printed page has always inspired a certain sense of unquestioning awe in people's minds. Combined with the recommendation of a respected teacher to the pliable minds of the young, it is little wonder that even children from Christian homes are convinced that when a textbook apparently contradicts the Bible, it still must be true.

In previous generations, parents trusted the textbooks as a part of the sacred establishment on the hilltop, and safely so, for the most part. But so much has changed, both in the "system" and in the books.

"John Nietz did a study of old textbooks and found that originally moral education was one of the principal objectives of our schools. According to Mr. Nietz, before 1775, religion and morals accounted for over 90 percent of the content of school readers. By 1926, this was down to 6 percent, and it is doubtless far less today, perhaps too small to be measured."[3]

Instead, many modern educational materials—books, movies, and audio-visuals—are saturated with a relative moral value system that encourages children to question everything they have been taught and look for "better" answers to life's questions.

Henry S. Myers, school board member and leader in the basics schools movement in Pasadena, California, says that there are two types of objectionable textbooks. One is the *dirty word type*. They are mostly English and supplementary literature books, such as *Go Ask Alice* and *Catcher in the Rye*. Some parents would include John Steinbeck's works in that category as well. Second, Mr. Myers identifies the *insidious types*.[4] That includes those books that present philosophies that undermine the work ethic, family values, parental authority, and respect for law and order. They may emphasize unhappiness, dissatisfaction, poverty, and injustice, especially for minorities and children. Others promote an anti-Christian approach to such issues as sex roles, treatment of handicapped and aged, drug usage, racial problems, and care of the environment.

Today it is imperative that we read at least parts of our children's textbooks for ourselves and find out what they are being exposed to. When we evaluate them, what objectionable features should we look for? Here are major problem areas:

• *Realism:* excessive amounts of profanity, sex, violence, protests, and crime presented as the accepted moral behavior patterns of modern society. One parent cited an example from one textbook of a sex orgy on a school bus. In the interests of realism, flaws of the heroes of American history may be played up almost to the exclusion of their virtues. True, we need to stop telling our children that the cherry tree myth is fact; but we also need to remind them that George Washington was a man of unusual integrity. Unfortunately, many children who have relied solely on the schools for their education have no sense of the horrors of Nazism and World War II, and see no ideological or practical objections to such things as Communism.

• *Situation ethics and behaviorism:* peer group consensus methods are applied to solving moral problems. Children are taught to question their parents' values and authority and to formulate their own moral philosophies based on a more contemporary system of value judgments. Very young children may have to decide when it is right to lie or to disobey parents. Teenagers may need to face the issues of smoking pot, living a gay life-style, or having an abortion.

• *Scientism:* an ideology that holds that knowledge of all kinds must be gained solely by means of the scientific method. Using that approach, textbooks present evolution as fact, while relegating creation to the mythological realms of religious ignorance. They ignore the increasing support of scientists for creation as a valid, scientific alternative explanation of origins.

• *Economic manipulation:* promoting the role of government in increasing control over the economy, while emphasizing the weaknesses of our free enterprise system.

• *Anti-Christian attitudes:* discounting the miraculous and supernatural element of Christianity and sometimes ridiculing those who take a strong Christian stand.

• *Occult, meditation cults, and so on:* courses on witchcraft, TM, and Eastern religious ideologies (see Appendix 9). I once worked with an English teacher who taught a form of meditation and encouraged students to write essays on witchcraft. The students found their library well-supplied with books on the subject.

• *Academic inferiority:* the lowering of reading grade levels of many textbooks to accommodate the lower abilities of students and/ or books that sacrifice academic quality in favor of psychiatric manipulation. Textbooks that do not challenge a student to expand his thinking and learning skills need to be protested by parents. One textbook producer wrote: "Our problem is that we can make better books than we can sell."[5] As in any other business, textbook companies must sell books to survive. If we parents can convince the educators, and through them the publishers, that we want the best they can produce, we will do a valuable service to the whole cause of upgrading educational quality.

• *Explicit sex education and alternative marriage styles exploration:* Some sex education programs are unbelievably explicit, even for the very young child. Reading excerpts of those materials is enough to make a parent ill. One such program was introduced into our county. Even though preview copies of the materials were sent to a select few educators with strict instructions that they were not to be copied or distributed, some local parents did secure copies. The materials were so atrocious that parents pressured the county superintendent to cancel training sessions for teachers. However, the battle is not over. Those persons and organizations (e.g., Planned Parenthood) that promote such programs do not give up easily.

It is difficult for most of us to imagine what motivates the educators who encourage the production of some of the more extreme forms of demoralizing books. Many thoughtful analysts are convinced that it is a key part of the campaign to subvert children's minds and thereby revolutionize the structure of our society. Perhaps that is true, though I am not ready to commit myself dogmatically to such a position. For me, the important issue is to recognize the satanic mastermind as the ultimate motivator behind it all. That allows me to fight the textbook battle while loving those persons who are Satan's tools and to see them as dear souls who have been duped by his convincing lies.

Before you grab your sword and rush pell-mell into an arena that for you may turn out to be nothing more than a cow pasture, let me offer a word of caution. In the Resource List I have referred you to a number of books and pamphlets that will help you in your battle to guard against inferior and dangerous textbooks. I will refer you to sources of textbook evaluation lists prepared by specialists in their field. Some lists evaluate the bad ones; others recommend good ones. You need, however, to know that not all textbooks are bad. In fact, you may find only a single objectionable book in a whole school. The problem with my telling you what is bad about schoolbooks is that you may tend to develop a negative attitude toward all the books and the whole system that purchases them. When the Holy Spirit through Peter told us to "be sober, be vigilant; because your adversary the devil, as a roaring lion, walketh about, seeking whom he may devour" (1 Peter 5:8), he did not intend for us to adopt a fanatical witch-hunting mentality. I cannot emphasize strongly enough the following four principles:

1. Not everything is wrong with any one school. There are no blanket facts that apply to every situation.

2. You can never accomplish the maximum for your child or your school unless you take a positive approach. Begin by looking for the books you can approve and support.

3. Every bad textbook, program, or teacher must be evaluated prayerfully to see whether our reaction should be one of protest, the offering of positive help, or the acceptance of the problem situation as a new type of training ground for both parents and child.

4. Do not let anybody else do your thinking or attitude setting for you. Until you have investigated a textbook or program firsthand and objectively, you are not ready to gird on your sword.

That there are problems with textbooks, we cannot deny. Specifically, what can we the parents do to insure quality and morality in this area? If you have chosen one of the alternative schools, especially if it is a church or Christian school, you may think that your textbook concerns are over. I wish I could tell you that that is automatically true. Indeed, alternative schools are less likely to use objectionable books, for those schools were founded to correct some of the felt ills of public schools. However, choosing such a school will never be a substitute for watchfulness in any area of education, including textbooks.

Whereas many alternative schools take precise care in making their textbook choices, others, struggling financially, may depend on public school castoffs to stock their shelves. One parochial school mother expressed concern that administrators were not too careful in making their choices. "There is too much salesmanship and not enough evaluating going on," she observed. "Many parents are busy and trust the schools too readily."

Even when Christian schools choose their books meticulously, we need to take a look. We should be no more accepting of a book that presents some radical denominational or doctrinal or "Christian cultural" viewpoint as absolute truth than one that promotes a humanistic philosophy. We need to teach our children to seek out truth instead of rigidly indoctrinating them to accept our ideas without question. We should not approve a book that is dull and unchallenging just because it is morally and doctrinally pure. When God's exciting truth is presented in a classroom or textbook in a dull fashion, it can actually have the effect of turning a child away from God.

Not all secular textbooks are inferior. Many are excellent. We can feel secure about using them in our church schools. Some teachers, by using godly wisdom, can actually use an inferior textbook to great advantage. By proper presentation and sufficient supplementing of the material, they can often turn it into an exercise in critical evaluation for the discovery of truth and the sharpening of independent study skills.

We need to be watchful and take action. But how? The principles discussed in chapter 9 apply here. In addition, there are several specific bits of advice from parents and experts in textbook evaluation.

First, *you may wish to fight the battle either alone or in a group.* Going it alone is the hard way, but if you cannot find a kindred spirit, do not hesitate to tackle it alone. Your PTA or Home and School Club may provide the logical structure through which to work. One couple in Texas told me that their high school PTA removed objectionable books. Their elementary PTA formed a parent textbook evaluation committee. You may need to form your own group. If you speak up about the things that concern you, wherever you are, you will usually find others who share your concerns. One group of politically active parents in Ohio serves as a parent lobby for decent textbooks at the state level. A history of responsible and fair action at local levels may win for you an appointment to your state textbook selection committee.

Whether individually or as a group, you need to observe the following rules if your battle is to be effective and still honor the name of Jesus Christ.

1. Be informed. A parent who dashes into a school board meeting and raves at the district officials about his emotional, negative reac-

tion to some book his child has told him about will probably not get anything like the kind of action he demands. Rather, his actions will tell the school board that he is one crackpot parent they need never listen to. If he makes the horrible error of telling them what church he comes from, he may succeed in putting the names of all his fellow-members on the blacklist with him.

To be informed, we must acquire the books and read them for ourselves. That is not always easy. Many classrooms do not have enough books to go around, and teachers hesitate to allow children to bring them home. My friend Nancy, of Citizens for Scientific Creation, suggests that, at the beginning of the school year, a parent should pay a friendly visit to the teacher. That helps to demolish "stranger" relationship barriers. You can tell her what your areas of concern are and offer to assist her in any way possible through the year. Be careful not to give the impression that you plan to spend the year sitting like an angry watchdog, glaring at her every move. Be certain that you do not *become* an angry watchdog.

During the year when you or your child discover areas that need checking, go to the teacher and, in kindness, ask permission to examine the textbooks in question. You may also ask to preview films to be shown in the classroom if you have reasons to believe that there are questionable segments. By all means, when the teacher invites you to a meeting to be briefed on something that is planned—be it a sex education program or a field trip to the opera—cancel everything else and *be there*.

Once you get the books or other materials, study them as thoroughly as needed in order to verify your objections. A brief scanning will usually reveal bad language. The more subtle problems will demand a more thorough reading. If you do not find in the textbook the problem that your child has alerted you to, check out the teacher's edition. You may find the problem in the goals and objectives section. Make notes as you read of all objectionable passages or words. Decide, usually by praying and discussing it with your mate, exactly why you object and how important the objections are.

2. Armed with all the facts, work through the established channels of your state or district. Go first to the teacher, then the principal, with your complaint. You may be told, "There is nothing we can do." When that happens, go to your district office and ask to see their written policy for requesting the elimination of objectionable ma-

terials. If that does not work, contact board members individually. Find out what procedure is used in your state and/or district for adopting textbooks and library materials. Regardless of established procedures, it is preferable to talk with individual board members, one at a time, before you bring your concern to an open board meeting for a public confrontation. Anything we can do to make it more comfortable for school officials to please us will increase our effectiveness.

3. Be fair. Do not ask your school board to remove the Koran from your library unless you are willing for a Muslim group to remove the Bible. It is not our duty to try to destroy pluralism in our democratic society. "The commission which Jesus Christ has left for His teachers is not to prevent the teaching of Darwinism or humanism or Hinduism but to 'go . . . teaching . . . all things whatsoever I have commanded you.' "[6]

4. Remember that it is easier to stop the adoption of a book than to get rid of it once it has been adopted. For more information on how to work effectively for textbook adoption, see Resource List.

5. The same principles apply in dealing with objectionable programs and classes (see Appendix 10). Several Indiana parents succeeded in preventing the introduction of classes in ESP, witchcraft, and other occult subjects. Concerned parents and US legislators worked to bring about a law prohibiting psychological testing of children without parental consent—a practice that was growing at one time.[7] By serving on district curriculum planning committees, school advisory councils and the like, we can have some important input in those areas as well.

The textbook arena is a hot and bloody battlefield. If we are to fight here, we must be particularly cautious to guard our living rooms, bedrooms, and kitchens at the same time. When we succeed in eliminating a values clarification program from a child's classroom, we can count on Satan to put extra pressure on us to run red lights on country roads, cheat on our income tax forms, and practice selfishness in the family circle. He knows that our inconsistency will do more to undermine our child's confidence in God's Word and the values we have taught him than all the values clarification classes in the world.

Obviously we cannot all engage in full-time combat on that one field, nor do we need to think that we must read every word of every textbook our child reads. After all, we cannot fully insulate him from life in the world. Furthermore, such action might easily turn us into angry watchdogs. However, we do need to read what we can and be alert for evidences that things are not going well.

Most important, we must keep the lines of communication open between us and our children. In today's high-pressure society, it is more vital than we often realize simply to help a child feel free to share with us the discrepancies he finds. Many teachers, anxious to get children to question their parents' values, are encouraging them to keep secret from Mom and Dad certain classroom proceedings and discussions of a moral nature. We must counter that challenge and keep our children talking. Only then can we prepare them to fight their own battles. When they open up to us, we can help them fill in the gaps, identify the problems, spot error when it is presented in a convincing form, and replace error with truth. That is, after all, what education is all about in the Christian home.

NOTES

1. John B. Conlan, Foreword, James C. Hefley, *Textbooks on Trial* (Wheaton, Ill.: Scripture Press, Victor, 1976), p. 5.
2. *Case Studies in Science Education*, booklet 15, "Knowing and Responding to the Needs of Science Education," University of Illinois, Urbana-Champaign, January 1978. Project for National Science Foundation.
3. Frank Goble, "Roots of American Disorder," newsletter, Thomas Jefferson Research Center (Pasadena, Calif.), June 1975, p. 2.
4. Henry S. Myers, Jr., *Fundamentally Speaking* (San Francisco: Strawberry Hill, 1977), pp. 44-45.
5. Frederick Seyforth, cited in Hillel Black, *The American Schoolbook* (New York: William Morrow, 1967), p. 24.
6. Christopher Hall, *The Christian Teacher and the Law* (Oak Park, Ill.: Christian Legal Society, 1975), p. 15.
7. Hatch Amendment. Educational Amendments of 1978 (PL 95-561).

12

VOLUNTEERS ARE VIPs

We are getting services on a volunteer basis that the tax-payer can't afford. . . . What's more, we are getting a relationship established between the community and schools.[1]

Linus Wright

"Once upon a time there were three Bears . . . One of them was a Little, Wee, Small Bear and one was a Middle-sized Bear, and one was a Great, Huge Bear . . ."

Ten fourth-grade girls squeezed together in a circle around one parent volunteer, Pat Tubbs, as she read a story that they knew well enough to recite in their sleep. As she read on, they cocked their heads in puzzlement, wrinkled their noses in disbelief, and burst into girlish giggles.

"We never heard it this way before!"

Mrs. Tubbs was sharing with her noon hour storytimers the original version of "Goldenlocks and the Three Bears." They were all making the exciting discovery that the story had changed considerably in the century or more since it was first introduced to somebody's children in England.

As a parent of two girls, she was part of an enthusiastic team of VIPs (Voluntary Involved Parents) in the early 1970s. The program was initially begun in 1968 at the Lakewood School in the Sunnyvale (Calif.) school district and was first called Parent Volunteer Aide Program. When the principal looked at the enormous task of his teachers he decided that they could use some help. In an environment where the increase of knowledge to be learned had reached a phenomenally explosive point, they were beginning to resemble two-legged octopuses facing eight-legged tasks. He had heard of using parents to assist with non-professional jobs. "Why not?" he asked. "The parents have been teachers ever since their own children were born."

So he handpicked a few teachers and parents who were eager to experiment. With the help of district personnel, he trained the parents in basic principles of math and reading education, matched them with teachers, and sent them out to work.

The project was a success from day one. The idea spread rapidly to other schools in the district. By the time I joined the volunteer ranks as a library helper at Lakewood School three years later, I discovered over five hundred parents, grandparents, and interested citizens working in our district's eighteen schools. I soon learned that we were only a tiny part of a huge cross-country movement of involved parents. From Maine to Hawaii and Florida to Alaska, we were all performing a variety of nonprofessional jobs. Functioning as the extra six legs of the octopus, we were freeing teachers to use their professional skills to a maximum benefit in the classroom.

For me, that was the beginning of a long volunteer career. Through the years since then as I have assumed many kinds of duties, I have also learned why being a VIP is so great, what it involves, and how to do it right.

First, why be a VIP? VIPs rarely have occasion to doubt their value. In fact, we feel like uniquely privileged people. How else could we have such close contact with the teachers in our children's schools? During the four years I worked in our school library, I got to know every member of the staff at least casually. I could talk to the teachers freely, and when I offered a suggestion or a word of praise, they knew it was genuine. By working as a part of the team on a volunteer basis, I proved that I cared about what went on at that campus.

Often I have heard an administrator or teacher say: "When I hear it from a parent, I pay attention." From experience I have found that by being on the scene I was able to gather information to validate my complaints, and as a result, I was more willingly heard.

Because volunteers know more about the operations of our schools, they are invaluable as rumor-control resources in the community. One education administrator from Princeton University, Donald Bagin, told a parent-teacher workshop that there are four questions parents most often ask about their schools. Dissatisfaction and false rumors usually result from improper answers to the following ques-

tions: What are they doing with our money? Are the students learning? Is the atmosphere disciplined? Are the schools as good as they
used to be?

Parent volunteers are in the best possible position to find accurate
answers firsthand. If the answers are unsatisfactory, we are right in
line to step up and get some action. Because we have actually seen
the facts, our knowledge is more respected and difficult to refute than
any rumor-based panicky fears expressed explosively at a school
board meeting. Many schools across the country have found that
volunteer parents are the best public relations people they have. In
the words of one administrator, "They are positive witnesses for an
institution that is maligned in the media and elsewhere." It is very
difficult to be overly critical of the team you work on.

For some parents, volunteer work leads eventually to paid positions
in the educational community. Today Pat Tubbs is a full-time specialist in gifted student programs for two district schools and a na-
tionally known computer instruction consultant. Many of our volunteer friends from the early 1970s have been hired as fulltime or
part-time classroom aides. Others became so excited with the process
and what they could do, that they went back to college, earned their
credentials, and are teaching today. Others of us have purposely
gone on volunteering and have experienced the opening of a new
world of intellectual curiosity and social stimulation.

At the same time, volunteer programs open up a whole community
of potential educational resources and put them at the disposal of our
students. They are also an economic asset. One teacher from Arizona
told me that volunteer helpers saved their district as much as several
thousand dollars per month. In addition, in one year volunteers raised
$3,000 for school projects.

I believe that, for me, the greatest benefit of being a volunteer
parent has been the way it has allowed me to be a part of my children's world. Because I have maneuvered my way through the halls
of Sunnyvale High School between classes, enroute to my classroom
aide assignment, rubbing shoulders with my children's peers, my
son's and daughters' world is familiar to me. I have smelled the cig-
arette smoke and watched the smiles and heard the banging of lockers
and spurts of laughter and foul language. I too have been jostled
through the crowd. I have felt the tension of hurrying to reach my
classroom before the tardy bell. On the way I have greeted a
growing number of friends—teachers, administrators, students (some

I had known since they were first and second graders). I have gone to the counselor, the school nurse, the learning center, the principal's office, the physical education locker room. I have parked my car in the student parking lot and observed the kinds of students who hang around the cars, place bottles behind wheels, cut classes. I have been there. I know a great many things that my children face—both good and bad. I understand their world a bit better. That helps me to know how to sympathize, how to advise, how to encourage, and how to prod when that is needed.

When I first became involved as a parent, I decided that as long as my children wanted to see me around their campuses, I would not disappoint them. I knew that the day would come when they would rather swallow castor oil. Until then I followed my youngsters through elementary, junior high, and high school always wondering when I would be asked to stay home. Strange to say, that day never came. In fact, one day I even stood in line at a local junior college to register my daughter for an orientation class, because she was out of state on the day it had to be done. My son has invited me to spend a week with him on his university campus doing research for a book I am planning.

One parent from Colorado shared with me that her son seemed genuinely proud that his mother worked in the school library. Knowing how terribly vital it is to a child's well-being and growth to be proud of his parents, I think that has to be the number one reason for being a volunteer.

What do VIPs do?

We are busy people who never exhaust our possibilities. Fifty years ago, parental involvement was restricted to room mothering, field trip chaperoning, and PTA membership. Today we can still find a place of usefulness in those areas. In fact, one of the major needs in parent volunteer ranks is for more active projects sponsored by PTA, Home and School Club, and other similar organizations.

The direction of those clubs is changing with our times. No longer do they restrict themselves to fund raising and sewing cushions for the faculty lounge. One PTA in Conway, Arkansas, led a workshop on "How to Develop Self-Esteem in Your Child" for community parents and teachers. Other groups too are sponsoring parent classes and seminars of many kinds. Often those same groups serve in the capacity of advisory committees to their schools. Sometimes they organize campus volunteer programs. One such PTA organized volunteer program grew into a city-wide, independent organization that furnishes volunteers, career education resources, and parent education for all the schools of the city.

Classroom aides do many things. They listen to students read in groups, assist in learning centers and health services, help with discipline, tutor students, supervise student activities, and dozens of other similar supportive tasks. In our increasingly cosmopolitan city population centers, many parents find useful opportunities as translators and interpreters. In our high school, we have students that speak many different languages—everything from Greek to rare Chinese dialects. One of our major needs is for persons who speak those languages to serve as aides in the counseling, bilingual, and English-as-a-second-language departments, as well as communicating with parents. That last function is very vital to the success of education for children from foreign-born homes.

In some cases, a volunteer may actually teach some portion of a subject under the teacher's supervision. I have done that type of work and found it immensely satisfying and fruitful. However, that is rare, except among paid aides. In some schools, parents work with students in a special program of discussing and reading through the Great Books program. I have worked with junior and senior high teachers in pull-out programs of special instruction of talented writing students.

Outside the classroom, the horizons are endless: library aides, playground supervisors, typists, telephoners, mailers, crafts helpers, paper correctors. Let your imagination run with this list. Some schools use parent volunteers to teach special interest extracurricular classes. I even have heard of one man who taught kayaking in a swimming pool on Saturdays.

A friend of mine worked with her principal, writing a weekly column for their small-town newspaper. In her column she informed the public about school events, problems, and achievements.

In some communities parents ride school busses to assist with discipline, especially during times of racial tension. Many parents serve on district advisory councils. One woman told me of a school scholarship committee. Begun as a project of the Business and Professional Women, it was taken over by a volunteer committee that now raises thousands of dollars in scholarship monies each year.

Career education and information centers are a growing part of many high school campuses. Often those are staffed at least in part by volunteers. I once knew a retired industrial arts teacher who took his turn each week in such a career center.

In one area, an organization called Music for Minors is funded by private sources and places volunteer music teachers in schools for a regular music enrichment program. Teachers are trained at the local junior college under a federal community grant. School and private volunteer groups sponsor similar programs in the other arts as well.

In addition to those regular kinds of involvement, many occasional projects need volunteer help and supervision as well. We all know about carnivals and picnics. But how about judging speech contests? School board electioneering? Campaigning for bond issues?

With the increased awareness of and emphasis on career education at all levels of school, many doors of involvement are open to parents to share their career, hobbies, or artistic or technical expertise in the classroom. One organization in Portland, Oregon, serves as a resource bank for such persons all over the area. It meets some surprising needs.

Unbelievable as it may seem, many children today grow up in homes where, apart from a bombardment with the mass media, their exposure to the world around them has been highly restricted. Volunteers function in a vital way in the lives of those youngsters. I first became aware of that situation when my junior high teacher friend and I took my writing group of eighth-grade girls on an observation trip to a nearby county park. In our valley area, located between two low mountain ranges, there are many such parks. We also live within easy driving distance of both the ocean and the Sierra Nevada. Those girls admitted that they had never visited such a place as that park before.

No matter what your circumstances, there is a place for you in the VIP ranks. As one Alaska teacher said, "There are places everywhere for the concerned Christian if he'll get off his halo and get his hands dirty."

Are VIPs welcome in the schools of America?

Usually the answer is yes. It is a rare school that does not allow the formation of a parent-teacher organization. Very few will refuse the assistance of parents outside the classrooms. When it comes to classrooms, we have another situation.

Most basics schools and some Christian and other private schools do not allow parents to serve in classrooms. They feel that extra adults in a classroom dilute the authority of the teacher. Apart from that, some teachers feel threatened by the presence of parents in the classroom. To them, the idea represents a censorship of their professional services by unqualified persons who have more of an emotional concern than an educational one. For every right way of doing a volunteer job, there is at least one wrong way. Some well-meaning parents manage instinctively to pursue all the wrong pathways and destroy the warm welcome with which they might otherwise be greeted.

One teacher from Georgia told me that their school had discontinued the use of volunteers. Why? Those they had tried had been undependable, inaccurate, sloppy, and negative. Some had even betrayed confidences and spread gossip.

What guidelines can a VIP follow in order to earn the commendation designated by a retired teacher from Washington state as the "ideal parent volunteer"?

1) *Be dependable.* Just because we do not punch a time clock is no excuse for not being there when we have promised to be. No program—volunteer or otherwise—can function with workers who only show up when they feel like it or have nothing better to do.

2) *Be adaptable.* A good volunteer follows directions, is sensitive to problems, and initiates helpfulness without getting pushy. We are here to serve, not to run things.

3) *Be professional.* Dress the part of a teacher. Hold confidences and remember that anything personal you learn about a child, staff member, or other parent is a confidence.

4) *Know the rules.* When you begin your volunteer work, you will probably be given an orientation and/or handbook that explains what is expected of you. Take your job seriously and abide by the rules.

5) *Ask questions.* If you do not understand something, ask (usually not during class, but at appropriate times). Get the facts and get them straight. Do not start rumors. If you see things that disturb you, talk with the teacher, your volunteer coordinator, or with the principal. Do not come on, swinging your sword. In fact, the classroom is one battlefield where you almost never need a sword.

6) *Respect the teacher.* Uphold her authority and integrity before the class. Do not try to compete with her for attention or respect. You are not competing in a popularity contest.

Serving as a VIP is rewarding. It is not always fun. It is sometimes frustrating, disappointing, or disillusioning. It may create problems or at least reveal them. It is one of the greatest opportunities we have. We cannot afford to bungle it.

Public education, private education—neither one can survive, much less thrive, without parental support and involvement. It always has been and always will be a joint effort. When it comes down to the bottom line, we VIPs—the Voluntarily Involved Parents of America—are key members of the regiments we join, in the battle for Quality Schools.

NOTE

1. "Troubled Schools Turn to Volunteer Helpers," *U.S. News and World Report*, 17 January 1977, p. 64.

13

PAID AND ELECTED INVOLVEMENT

The final decision of what goes into the schools rests with the lay boards of education. . . . The schools do belong to the people and the schools are an extension of the home and community . . .[1]

John Navarra

As IMPORTANT AND SATISFYING as the VIP role may be, for some of us there comes a day when we will step out of the volunteer ranks to assume a different kind of role. The opportunity and the challenge present themselves, and we know that the time is right to become a professional educator.

Mrs. R_____ was one of these. She had lost several babies. Then God gave her a healthy, normal daughter. She poured her life into that special child's development. When the girl started kindergarten, her mother enlisted as a volunteer. "She was the model volunteer parent," her teacher recalls. Through the years, she followed Tammy through school. Finally she enrolled in college, got her teaching certificate, and became a professional teacher.

Mrs. K_____ was another. When her child was in high school, she did some volunteer publicity writing. District administrators were impressed with her work and hired her to serve as their professional public relations person.

Mrs. B_____ got her start as a classroom aide. Finding things she wanted to change, she began to work through appropriate channels and ended up at school board meetings, speaking her mind. There she learned more about the educational machinery. The political aspects of education intrigued her, and she became a regular attender at the monthly meetings. Soon she was picked to serve on district committees. Finally she ran for a school board position and got it. Today, in addition to her local school board duties, she holds offices in both state and national school board associations.

Professional educators fall into two main categories: *salaried* educators and *elected or appointed* educators. The average parent thinks of educators as the *salaried* persons only. Making up the people we meet on the campuses of our schools are: teachers, paid aides, administrators, librarians, custodians, secretaries, psychologists, and counselors. There are others we may not be aware of, though. Most of them work in the district offices, which we rarely visit. A whole host of consultants, specialists, district superintendents, financial advisers, coordinators, public relations people, and dozens of others keep the machinery running. In addition, many communities have independent professional organizations that educate parents, run volunteer programs, or perform consulting and other vital services to the educational community.

Preparing for one of those salaried positions involves meeting the educational requirements that vary with the job and state, local, or private school policies. Many parents are already educated to do the jobs they assume. For some, it will mean a return to the classroom as a student to get the necessary training. I know two women who stepped quite naturally into their positions as liaison persons between an English-speaking school and the Spanish-speaking population that they represented. All they needed was a bit of specialized training by the school district.

Perhaps the most important qualification for professional educators is attitude—a love for children, patience, ability to work well under stress, and positive attitudes toward parents. As one administrator summarized it, a school staff needs to adopt the philosophy that "people are more important than things."

Men as well as women are always needed in the educational world—especially in elementary classrooms. That becomes increasingly important as more and more children come from homes without fathers. Many children have a distorted view of manhood. To some of them, a man is an undesirable person who gets drunk, beats his wife and children, or simply ignores his family. As one girl told her friend: "I wouldn't want a father. They're more trouble than they're worth." For others, a man is the jolly, absentee father who comes for periodic visits. He always brings treats, has fun with the child, overindulges him, and almost never administers discipline.

Every child needs exposure to a caring and capable man. The school janitor may be one of the best-loved people on campus. Two reasons are that he often projects a warm father image and that he can always fix everything. Good men teachers share that sort of respect and affection. I have seen it happen, and it is truly special.

Should mothers of young children move into the salaried ranks? Volunteering allows a mother the freedom to serve on a schedule, but be absent when necessary to care for her children. Salaried jobs are a bit more restrictive. In many areas of our society, that question is considered to be quite old-fashioned. The *in* thing today is for every woman to work, regardless of the ages of her children. In many cases, it does become a necessity.

Meanwhile, children's needs have not changed with the times. Every child still needs to come home to a mother who is there, cheerful, and alert enough to be available to spend as much time with him as his needs demand. More often than not, our children need us most at that special moment when they walk in the door. The world outside is never quite so friendly to them as Mother can be. A mother's role as educator at home involves being an encourager, a listener, a healer. To perform that role, she must be on duty.

Many mothers find jobs in education to be well-suited to the schedule needs of their growing families. If their hours can coincide with the children's hours, the situation can be nearly ideal. Some paid aide positions are only part-time, and the mother can choose her hours. When a professional educator's job absorbs so much of a mother's time and energy that she must give her family leftovers of herself, it is time to take a second look at circumstances, priorities, and one's standard of living.

The second category of professional educators is the large group of *elected and appointed officials.* They are the political policy makers that determine who will teach what and with what resources. There, we find state superintendents, commissioners, or secretaries of education (or instruction). In eighteen states, those people are elected. In other states, they are appointed by either the state board of education or the governor. All states except Wisconsin have state boards of education. They are elected in twelve states and appointed in the others. Those state officials are the chief administrators responsible for working with state legislators to make policies and oversee the smooth operation of the schools. Until recently when the federal government began legislating itself into the field, states have been given almost total responsibility for education—a responsibility they have shared with county and local district organizations. Today, we also have a cabinet level Department of Education in Washington, D.C., with regional offices around the country.

Special committees function with appointed and/or paid members at all levels. States, for example, have textbook selection committees. Districts and local campuses use citizen committees for everything from general advisory work to researching compliance with desegregation regulations. Even the federal government works through citizen committees, such as the White House Conference on Families.

The political body that parents are usually most familiar with is the local school board, often called a board of trustees or school committee. This community group of generally three to eleven members, is the policy-making body for a school district. Normally, members are chosen by popular vote in nonpartisan elections, but some are appointed either by city mayor or a panel of judges. In years gone by, the real power in education lay mostly with those boards of local citizens. I can remember when many school campuses had their own school boards and parents took an active part in their proceedings.

Today the school board has lost many of its administrative powers to the district superintendent and state boards of education. Their function is primarily to pass resolutions that establish policies; plan budgets; approve curriculum; oversee financial matters; and sometimes handle assigning, hiring, and firing of personnel.

Private schools of all kinds have their school boards. If your children attend any of the alternative schools, investigate thoroughly to discover who sets school policies and how. Is there perhaps a place for you to serve in that capacity? How much voice would you have? What is involved in becoming a member of that decision-making body?

How much power do school boards have today? The answer depends upon whom you talk with. One superintendent from New York State says, "The State legislature has mandated so many things now that there's not really much choice on the local level." In the same state, however, one school board banned eleven school books from the library. When angry parents and students took them to court for what they called "unjustifiable censorship," they decided that the board had a lot of power, for the courts upheld the board's right to decide whether school library books were fit for students to read.

In California, I have talked with school board members who are frustrated by demands of state-mandated programs and/or strong district administrators. One woman board member told me that boards are losing control because they have not been politically active. She believes that they need to move into the lobbying roles at state and national levels. At the same conference where I met that woman, though, I heard dozens of stories about school boards that have fought the new basics education schools fiercely. They have only failed because of the persistence and creative financial planning of the parents and teachers who insist on keeping those schools open at any cost.

"It is a continual fight!" That testimony was repeated over and over, indicating that the school boards at least have the power to make parents very miserable with the continuation of the thing they have demanded.

How can a parent prepare to become a school board member? In talking with a variety of educators and board members, I have accumulated the following suggestions. Regardless of whether you are looking at a public school or private school board position, the following tips should help you to decide whether this is a battlefield where you might put your talents and ideas to work:

1. Get acquainted with the schools in your district. Spend time on campuses (not just your own), at the district offices, and at board meetings. If possible, work as a volunteer in a variety of capacities throughout your district.

2. Build a strong political support base in your community. Get acquainted with your community and its political climate. Visit City Hall and town meetings. Join neighborhood concern groups. Solicit people's opinions about educational issues in the grocery store and the barber shop. Practice the art of being sensitive to the ideas of your supporters.

3. Learn everything you can about education. Keep up to date on current issues and trends. Books, papers, magazines, reports, legislative records—read them all. I heard of one board member, a chemist, who read so much about all phases of education that he actually knew more than some of the professional educators in his district.

4. Get involved in committee work. Make a visible contribution to the political education process that will obviously qualify you to do more.

5. Develop your own clearly worded educational philosophy. Try

to determine what is the philosophy of members of your community as well. Remember that you have the responsibility to represent community feeling, so you need to learn how to find out what that feeling is.

6. Get to know your legislative representatives. They are the people who will make the laws that you as a board member must live with. Let them know your concerns, how many people support you, and how your community feels about educational issues.

7. Learn to deal with people and compromise on non-essentials for the accomplishment of community goals. One principal observed that some people get elected to school board positions, expecting to make immediate changes in everything. If they have a teachable spirit at all, however, they soon learn what the real problems are that face elected officials, and they gain a new sympathy for both educators and education.

8. As a Christian, pray a lot. Ask God for that rare combination of a gentle spirit and the ability to stand by your firm convictions. Ask Him to help you be realistic before you make campaign promises and then to carry through in a way that is both honorable and practical. Above all, ask Him to enable you to protect His image in your community. Although you may be representing the people who elect you to office, you are representing the kingdom of God and the King of the universe.

With that kind of preparation, the cooperation of your family, and the clear leading of the Holy Spirit, you can enter the school board battlefield with utter confidence. "Faithful is he that calleth you, who also will do it" (1 Thessalonians 5:24).

Several years ago our high school vice-principal assigned me to do some editing work on a school accreditation report. I welcomed the opportunity to get better acquainted with every area of the school and many of the teachers and to learn a bit more about morale among staff members. Once he had given me the details of my new volunteer assignment, he smiled and said tentatively: "I don't know exactly what I am trying to do—maybe to prepare you to become a school board member?"

That dear man did not know me as well as I knew myself. I love to be involved voluntarily. I will gladly do a dozen things around campus. I will even attend board meetings occasionally and serve on a school site council. But enter the political arena? No way! One of the things I definitely lack is a political aptitude. In fact, I detest politics. With my attitude, I could never even win an election. If I did, I would be totally devastated, perched up there in that school board cage, flanked by district administrators and faced by sometimes hostile parents, teachers, and students.

By the same token, I have not yet been willing to fill any of the salaried positions that have been offered to me. Perhaps the day will come. But if it never does, that makes me no less a committed supporter of good schools for my community's children.

There is always going to be one thing I need to do for education, no matter how old I grow, nor how far removed I may be from the need for education for my children. That same privilege and duty is shared by every adult citizen of our nation. As registered voters, we have the obligation to help elect those board members, legislators, state school superintendents, and even presidents and vice-presidents who will protect what we believe are the essential elements of a quality and morally safe education. As one author says, "If politics is the art of allocating scarce resources to meet unlimited needs, then we need to pay more attention to the process of *who* decides *what*."[2]

We always need to look for candidates (1) whose philosophy of education parallels our own as much as possible, (2) who will support the freedom of alternative schools, (3) who consider education as a high priority item for legislative consideration, (4) who protect parental and student rights and responsibilities in education, and (5) who, whether Christian or non-Christian, are honest, trustworthy, dedicated, and in every way qualified to do their job well.

NOTES

1. Hillel Black, *The American Schoolbook* (New York: William Morrow, 1967), p. 22.
2. James J. Gallagher and Patricia Weiss, *The Education of Gifted and Talented Students: A History and Prospectus* (Washington, D.C.: Council for Basic Education, 1979), p. 34.

14

OUR NEEDS ARE SPECIAL

What we really mean when we declare our dedication to equality is not equality of results, but equality of opportunity."[1]

Lawrence L. Orr, Jr.

EVERY CHILD IS SPECIAL—a unique individual with his own set of abilities, strengths, weaknesses, and problems. Most children fall into a number of fairly predictable, scientifically catalogued patterns of learning and behavior. The thing that makes each one unique is his one-of-a-kind combination of common patterns with the God-given spark we call personality.

Some children, however, are more special than they are average. Their distinctive qualities affect their living and learning processes to such an extent that they require special attention in order to gain an effective whole-person education. *Exceptional children,* they are sometimes called.

Exceptional children fit in many categories. Some are mentally retarded; others are mental geniuses. Some have physical handicaps; others are unusually gifted in athletics or mechanics. Some have emotional and psychological disorders that prevent them from normal learning; others demonstrate high levels of artistic creativity and/or leadership capacity. Exceptional children, with all their differences, are broadly classified either as *handicapped* or *gifted.*

It has been estimated that 10 percent of all children are handicapped—physically, mentally, or emotionally—to such an extent that they cannot learn well in the average classroom setting. Others suffer from slight handicaps that do not hinder learning so much. The number of identified handicapped children is expanding rapidly today—

particularly in the emotional and learning disability categories. According to a National Institute of Health study, between 11 and 22 percent of today's children enter school with such a high degree of emotional damage that they are incapable of learning little more than to read and write.[2]

At the other end of the spectrum, children in the various gifted groups—mentally gifted, artistically creative, having leadership potential, and athletically or mechanically gifted—constitute somewhere between 2 and 5 percent of the school population.

Many parents would like to think their child's specialness puts him in the gifted class. Most are happy to have average, normal, healthy children who are special just because of who they are in their families. Rarely does a parent wish for a handicapped child of any kind. In fact, many feel it is some sort of disgrace to have a handicapped child. Some believe that God is judging them in some way by giving them a deformed or retarded child. Others refuse to admit that their child could be handicapped. After all, does not God give the best to His children? How difficult it is for all of us to recognize that our trials and disappointments are God's special messengers to teach us patience and faith in Himself. We can be sure that if God sends us a handicapped child, He has given us the best.

When it comes to emotional and behavioral handicaps, the tendency among Christians is to look at the increasing numbers of learning-disabled children and shake our pious heads. "The harvest of the drug generation, disintegrating families, and moral laxness," we smugly state. When we see such a child from a Christian home, we whip out a file of pat recipes for such "ungodly" problems—more discipline, more dedication of parents, better spiritual training. To many it is unthinkable that good Christian homes should have those kinds of problem children.

I used to feel a bit this way myself. Then one summer evening, I arrived at a church meeting early to discover a friend reading a book with a title something like *How to Handle Your Overactive Child.*

What is she doing with that? My reaction was immediate. Then I remembered that she and her husband were raising a foster child with severe emotional problems gained from an obviously non-Christian background. My naive logic did not prepare me for what happened during the next fifteen minutes. As others arrived—all godly, stable, respectable Christian parents—they caught a glimpse of the book and exclaimed with an unbelievable eagerness: "Let me see that book. Do I ever need it!" In no time my friend had a sizable circle of parents (not foster parents) clustered around her relating frustrations. I went home that night with a very different outlook on the whole subject.

All our lives we have been taught that Jesus Christ can solve our problems—and indeed He can! We mistake that to mean that we can automatically expect our homes to be exempt from major problems. Those expectations might be close to logical if we all had:

1. *Perfect parents*—each possessing the mature character of God, the unique gifts of understanding and communicating with children that the parenting books tell us about, and the educational expertise of the model teachers we remember from our nostalgically tinted past.

2. *Perfect children*—obedient, little rubber-stamp models always submissive to the pressure exerted on them by godly home training.

3. *Perfect environment*—a world that is friendly to God and with an atmosphere that nurtures stable emotional and psychological growth.

The truth is, however, that our parents were imperfect and inexperienced and raised us in less-than-perfect homes. We were imperfect and often unresponsive to their training. Our world was neither a friend to God nor to stability of character. Consequently, we too begin parenting with imperfect homes and imperfect children in an imperfect world. We should not be surprised to learn that Christian families (sometimes even our own) need special education facilities for our hyperactive, emotionally disturbed and/or learning-disabled children.

It helps to realize that many different factors contribute to creating the learning handicaps of our children. Most of them have nothing to do with our spirituality or even the level of our parental expertise. One specialist lists the following factors:[3]

1. "Intelligence." Each child is born with a set of intellectual equipment waiting to be developed. Some children, when given the proper encouragement, grow far beyond normal expectations for their intelligence level. However, wise parents recognize that each child has limits imposed on him by his innate capacities and learn to work with those limitations creatively.

2. "Sensory deficits." Not all children's senses are equally sharp. Many have deficiencies in one or more areas that keep them from learning at the rate and in the ways we consider normal.

3. "Activity level and attention span." All children have a higher activity level and shorter attention span than normal adults. Some never seem to stop running, jumping, wiggling, or wandering about. They do not concentrate on anything for more than an extremely short time.

4. "Brain injury and minimal brain dysfunction (MBD)." Research in that area is a relatively young science and not too much is known. But it does seem certain that there is some connection between brain injury and learning.

5. "Genetic factors." Learning problem areas may be, at least in part, inherited. This is closely related to the inheritance of talents, abilities, and temperamental characteristics.

6. "Immaturity." For many reasons children do not all mature at the same rate. Based partly on that fact, one popular school of thought advocates that some children be allowed to start school at a later age than is traditional. Correct timing in that area can mean the difference between success and failure for some children. In the September before our son turned six (in late December), we put him in a parochial school. One of the first questions the principal asked when I went for the application interview was: "Are you coming to us because the public school won't take him in the first grade until he is six? Or are you interested in kindergarten?"

When I assured her that we were asking for kindergarten, she smiled her relief. "So many parents make the big mistake of pushing their children into first grade before they are ready," she explained. "They get off to a bad start and spend the rest of their school days never being quite able to keep up."

7. "Emotional factors." Children's emotions are very sensitive. A child who is always failing and never succeeding learns to fear reaching out to learn new things. Risk becomes too painful for him to accept. An average child with gifted siblings may experience unhealthy fears of failure and lack of self-worth. A strong spirit of competition between children in a family can be destructive. Children are susceptible to the pressure of parental expectations. Social anxieties also play a role. One child will learn to sacrifice academic performance if he thinks such action will bring him more social acceptance. Another will retreat into his books and stop trying to cope with society.

8. "Environmental factors." The insecurities of Western society place severe pressures on our children. Medical experts and educa-

tors are examining many of the key elements of our culture as prob-
able contributors to the increase in learning disabilities. Things like
improper nutrition, food additives, and prepackaged foods; indus-
trialization with its attendant noise, pollution, "workaholism," and
depersonalization; the mass media; and a cancerous growth of anti-
authoritarian attitudes expressed by the many "lib" movements—all
are highly suspect.

When we use the term *handicapped* in education, we refer to children who are in any way incapacitated or hindered from functioning
and learning as their peers do—for example, physically disabled,
emotionally unstable, brain damaged, mentally retarded, and so on.

Until recent years many of those children were denied the right to
be adequately educated at public expense. Some physical handicaps
created difficulties no one knew how to deal with in the regular classroom. Children with mental and emotional handicaps were considered either discipline problems or uneducable. Today the attitude
has changed drastically. One superintendent of schools, agreeing
with Council for Basic Education, summarized the current philosophy of educators on the matter: "Every child has a right and a
capacity to learn."[4]

The change in thinking about handicapped children has come
about through the persistence of parents and teachers who refused
to accept the "undisciplined" or "uneducable" philosophy. Many experiments in handicapped education were carried on in private institutions. As parents saw those programs work, they knew that the old
diagnoses were mythological. They began challenging, in court, their
states' refusal to provide education for their children. Those court
cases led to state programs of special education and eventually to the
passage by the federal legislature of the Education for all Handicapped Children Act of 1975 (PL 94-142). According to that law,
states must provide a "free appropriate education" for all handicapped children. Among other things, the law provides for the following:

1. Children will be educated in regular classrooms wherever possible, rather than being shoved into the nearest class for retarded or
learning disabled students.

2. Parents must be notified of any proposed changes in their children's education.

3. Parents must be included in the writing of an Individualized

Education Plan (IEP) for each child and in periodically reviewing the progress of that plan.

4. The federal government will partially fund the administration of that program as long as the state and local district comply with all regulations in the law.

PL 94-142 addresses a great need. It is not without problems, however. Being a federally funded program, it comes with strings attached and restrictions that cannot possibly apply to all circumstances without adjustment. Some educational analysts see it as a threat to the economic structure of the public school system and to the freedoms of the very children and parents for whom the bill was intended. Inadequate available local funds make compliance with the law difficult. Some states are attempting to avoid adoption of the law by refusing federal funds and establishing their own special education programs. Many parents are having difficulty getting all the things the law promises them. Educators are finding the mountain of paperwork and overtime hours required for full compliance to be unrealistic. Undoubtedly PL 94-142 will face many revisions and updating in the future; it has undergone some already. Parents who care about the implementation of the law should become politically involved in this arena.

One thing is certain. The law is with us and is not likely to be repealed. Hence, regardless of how we feel about it, we must learn to live with it. In the Resource List, you will find a listing of materials to help you untangle the miles of red tape and make the law work for you and your child.

What can we expect the schools to do for us and our handicapped children? Basically, the schools do three things.

First, *they help us to identify a child's learning difficulites*. Physical and severe mental handicaps are obvious. But how do we know whether a child is really hyperactive, emotionally disturbed, brain damaged, or borderline retarded? Sometimes those problems may be confused with normal activity, immaturity, social reticence, or some physical handicap. Usually the answer can only be determined by professional diagnostic testing and analysis of psychologists or physicians.

This book is not the place to discuss the symptoms of learning disabilities. If I gave you a list, you would probably panic. The symptoms are many and, taken singly, are typical of child behavior at certain stages of development. We all can find our children on such a list at some points. Suffice it to say here that if your child exhibits habitual patterns of questionable behavior and nonlearning, you should discuss those patterns with your pediatrician and teacher.

Have the child go through a complete physical, including a thorough check of vision and hearing. Talk with his teacher. If after conferences and examinations you still have reason to suspect that there is a genuine problem, ask the teacher for a referral to the school psychologist for testing. Your request to have your child tested must be granted, even if the teacher believes it is unnecessary. Anyone—parents, student, teacher, or other educator—can request those tests. However, they cannot be administered before you, the parent, sign a permission form. According to the law, from the time you sign those papers the psychologist has forty-five working days to do the tests and bring a report to you, the parents. Within thirty working days of the psychologist's diagnosis, your child must be situated in a new classroom if the analysis indicates that such a change is necessary.

Second, *the school helps you plan a course of action to deal with your child's identified handicap.* The law mandates that you (or some person you designate) must take part in the planning process. Since you may not be an educator yourself, you need to be aware of your limitations in understanding all that is involved and trust the professional wisdom of the educators on the team. That will mean getting acquainted with the members of the team and developing a relationship of cooperative trust. You alone know things about your child that the educators need to know in order to help them put together the best possible IEP. It will be vital for you to tell them anything that you believe might be even remotely pertinent.

At the same time, read all that you can about the subject. Contact a local group of parents of handicapped children. If there is not one in your area, write to one of the national or state organizations listed in the Resource List. Those parent groups are extremely helpful. Here you gain strength from the supportive attitudes and practical advice of other parents who know your feelings and have been grappling with the same frustrations you may have believed were yours alone.

Finally, *the school will help you place your child in the best learning situation for him.* Some children need a special education class, either all day every day or for a part of each day. Other children function well in a regular classroom with an occasional visit to a resource room where they receive special instruction in areas of their disabilities. The process of integrating handicapped children as much as possible into nonhandicapped classes is called *mainstreaming* and is the approach favored by most educators and the law today. It does not work for all children, however, and may seriously hinder learning for other children in the regular classroom.

Parents can create problems for themselves and their children when it comes to placement. We naturally want our children to be normal. When that desire keeps us from admitting that a child needs special help, we only fool ourselves and keep him from realizing the potential he has. One pair of educators offers a guiding principle: "If your child is not and cannot be an accepted member of his natural peer group, spare him the pain of being an outsider. Find an environment where he can adapt."[5]

On the other hand, some parents, in their eagerness to give a handicapped child all the help he can get, may push to have him placed in a special class, when all he needs is a bit of special assistance in a regular class. Such identification of a child as handicapped can destroy his self-image and as Haim Ginott warned, "the diagnosis becomes the disease."

Because the whole area of special education is relatively new, especially in some school districts, you may have difficulty getting the help and cooperation you need. A friend of mine who has adopted several handicapped children with various needs had that experience. As a result, she and her husband studied the law themselves and learned about and pursued all the legal resources open to them. She suggests that parents keep a complete file of information on each child. Include all correspondence with the school, notes from teachers, doctors, everything that could have any bearing in the case. You might need it all.

Regardless of how well-equipped the school may be to handle the needs of your handicapped child, they cannot do it all. As with all children you, the parent, still hold the key to the success of his education. That involves at least three basic things:

1. *An accepting attitude.* "The most common mistake . . . is to panic when you discover that your child is not perfect."[6] Instinctively, we feel that a child's imperfection somehow reflects our character flaws. Of all people, we Christians should be able to erase that erroneous idea. The handicapped child is a gift from God, entrusted to our care for some very loving reasons that we may not yet understand.

Through that child, we may have the opportunity to experience glimpses of God's love and tenderness and the simplicity of faith that we could never gain through all the normal children in the world. By our attitude and some conscious reaching, we can help the child to accept himself for the special person that he is. One teacher of missionaries' children observed that when the handicapped child's parents were unaccepting of his problem and were nervous about it, the child had even more difficulty learning to cope with his handicap. As one woman said: "He is after all, just a child with a difference in the way he learns. He's not a learning difference with a child attached."[7]

2. *A structured home life with a good balance of affection and firm discipline.* The handicapped child needs the security provided by a structured schedule and atmosphere and clear expectations. We need to lay down realistic rules of moral conduct and responsibility and enforce them consistently. As parents, it is imperative that we agree on those things and work as a united team. We must make sure that he gets a good breakfast *every* morning, eats dinner at the same time *every* day, gets a warm bath, a goodnight kiss, and ten hours of sleep *every* night. We need to resist the temptation to overindulge him because we feel sorry for him and find firmness too difficult.

3. *An active, observable faith in God and lots of positive, spiritual training.* No matter how handicapped or retarded a child may be, he should be taught about both the love and demands of God. Include him in family worship. Let him take his turn leading in prayer, sharing ideas, helping with family art and missionary projects. Do all the things to nurture his spiritual development that you do for your other children. Add the extras he may need as well.

Spend time in prayer for the needs of that child. Avoid the temptation to give to the special child so much time and energy in both prayer and involvement that you neglect the rest of your family (especially your mate) and your own needs. The goal is to keep things as normal as possible. At times when the whole family needs to help meet the needs of your special child, encourage them. Also encourage the handicapped child to help when one of the other family members needs concentrated family attention.

Is your child more special than ordinary? Thank the Lord for him and ask Him to show you creative ways to turn his handicap into a learning asset for the whole family. Like Paul, parents of handicapped children can learn to say, "Most gladly therefore will I glory in my infirmities that the power of Christ may rest upon me" (2 Corinthians 12:9).

NOTES

1. *San Jose Mercury,* 13 November 1979.
2. Jeannette Elpel, "Crisis of Ineffective Parenting," *Sunnyvale* (Calif.) *Scribe,* 7 February 1979, p. 16.
3. Betty B. Osman, *Learning Disability—A Family Affair* (New York: Random House, 1979), pp. 18-24.
4. Johnny L. Jones, "CBE Elects," *Basic Education,* November 1979, p. 9.
5. Stella Chess, M.D., with Jane Whitbread, *How to Help Your Child Get the Most Out of School* (Garden City, N.Y.: Doubleday, 1974), p. 256.
6. Chess and Whitbread, p. 164.
7. Osman, p. 155.

15

OUR NEEDS ARE SPECIAL TOO

The parent of the gifted child has a very special opportunity to broaden the learning horizons of . . . a potential leader of our country; a future scientist; an award-winning writer; or one of many accomplished and notable figures.[1]

Herbert Kanigher

PARENTING A GIFTED CHILD can be a rewarding, exciting, and challenging adventure, or it can be a frustrating disappointment. The gifted child is blessed with unusual potential to become a leader of his generation in government, medicine, the creative arts, science, industry, invention, counseling, athletics, or in whatever area his giftedness lies.

If all goes well, and he responds to the inner proddings of his gifts and the external encouragement of wise parents and teachers, his parents will run proudly beside him until he outruns them and takes his place at the head of his society. If all does not go well, his parents may watch him retreat into a corner, letting his gift shrivel and die while he flounders his way through life at the bottom of the heap. Worse yet, he may develop his gift to the fullest and excel by all the world's standards, while ignoring the God who gifted him and never reaching the spiritual potential his parents value as first in importance.

Teaching the gifted child can be either rewarding, exciting, and challenging, or it can end in frustration and disappointment. *Time* (23 April 1979) tells the story of a gifted boy named Tommy. "He is the kind of child a teacher dreams of having once in a lifetime," his principal said. "But now that we have him, we don't know what to do with him."

147

His perplexed educators thought he was a behavior problem, but then decided that he had a learning disability. Testing showed that he had an IQ of 169. They shoved him into a twelve-week program for gifted children where he was exposed to mostly arts and crafts and some field trips run by a volunteer. Finally, the school gave him permission to enroll in a high school Spanish class; but the school board revoked the permission, because they thought it would set an undesirable precedent. That brought Tommy and his teachers back to square one.

If we think parenting and teaching a gifted child are rough, what about *being* that child? Someone has accurately assessed the frustrations of giftedness among children in this statement: "Sometimes . . . it's hard to be a peacock when you want to be part of the flock of sparrows."[2] Often a gifted child will ignore the demands of his giftedness and perform at the average level or below, just in an attempt to become "one of the sparrows."

The attitude of society toward gifted persons in America is a mixed one. It has been described as a "love-hate relationship."[3] We revere gifted persons who have raised themselves from unlikely beginnings and contributed substantially to the progress or leadership of society; but we hesitate to give the gifted child any special attention, so as to encourage the creation of an elite class of intellectual snobs. We do not hesitate to reach down and help lift the handicapped child up to our level of normalcy—but to help a child climb beyond our reach? Somehow that threatens our sense of security, and we subconsciously rationalize away our duty to such children. This is evidenced by the way our society appropriates funds for education. For example, in Tommy's state $740 per year is spent on each of the 220,000 handicapped students, while only $40 goes to each of the 70,000 gifted students.

Many people try to excuse this imbalance by assuming that a gifted child's inner compulsions are so strong that he is bound to make it on his own without special assistance or encouragement. Sounds great, does it not? We can even point to men like George Washington Carver and Abraham Lincoln who did just that. But for every Carver or Lincoln that made it, there were hundreds (maybe thousands) with equal and perhaps more recognizable promise who dropped out and went to a nameless or an infamous grave.

Some related statistics are quite revealing. Recent government

research tells us that 35 percent of high school dropouts were enrolled in special education (handicapped) classes in elementary
school. That is not necessarily surprising. At the same time Dr. Harold Lyon, former Director of Health, Education, and Welfare's Office
for the Gifted and Talented, says, "Almost 30 percent of the dropouts
are gifted and talented youth."[5] That is particularly significant when
we consider that handicapped students represent about 10 percent
of the population and the gifted represent only between 2 and 4
percent. Furthermore, the highest suicide rate of students is from
the gifted group, with gifted girls rating highest of all.

Giftedness is no guarantee of success, no matter how you define
success. In fact, in our society where gifted children are largely
unappreciated by their peers, neglected by the taxpayers, and mis-
understood by the average people that most influence their lives,
giftedness has become a kind of handicap.

Before we go further, we need to define the term *gifted,* now usually expanded to include *gifted and talented.* The US Office of Education has identified six different areas where a child may give evidence of unusual ability. In order to be categorized by the educational system as gifted and talented, a child must excel in at least
one of these ability areas. Most fit into two or more of them. They
are:

- General intellectual ability—the all-around bright child
- Specific academic aptitude—the math or science whiz
- Creative or productive thinking—the child who comes up with
novel solutions to problems
- Leadership ability—initiates and leads games and groups
- Ability in the visual or performing arts—painting, music, drama,
and sculpture
- Psychomotor ability—athletic ability and mechanical skills[6]

Giftedness goes beyond the above classifications, however, to a
child's way of learning or his approach to life. As one parent put it,
those children generally "do things a little earlier, a little better,
a little more quickly, and a little bit differently from other children."[7]
It is important to be aware that some gifted children may at first
appear to be slow learners or hopeless daydreamers. "Very often
the brightest students will take the longest time to do a piece of
homework that involves creativity because they are aware, as a less
able student would not be, of the many possibilities it offers for
interesting accomplishment and pleasure."[8] Speed does not tell it

all. Einstein did not even speak until he was four years old or learn to read until he was seven. Thoroughness, ability to stick with a difficult project to completion, and a wide variety of interests can be equally valid indicators of giftedness as well as speed and early accomplishment.

If you believe your child is gifted, check with your school or some of the materials suggested in the Resource List. Again, it is not our purpose here to list all the indicators of giftedness. Inaccurately identifying the gifted child can be as dangerous as mislabeling a handicapped child.

In our home, we never heard of gifted programs or classifications until our older daughter was in the fourth grade. Her teacher recommended her for inclusion in the gifted program of that year. Although she had not been tested and identified as gifted, she was obviously gifted in music. Since the program emphasis for the district for that year was music, she was included. Later, a sixth-grade teacher identified our son as gifted. He had been slow showing an interest in the learning process, but once he began, he could not be stopped. Our younger daughter was never tested, but she too showed unusual talents in the performing and musical arts. Teachers and counselors came to the assistance of all our children and helped them find the school programs that best suited their talents. Some of the programs were special, accelerated programs designed for the gifted. Others were not. They all found ample opportunity to develop those areas in which they were especially gifted.

Not all school districts pay such close attention to the individual needs of gifted children. Unfortunately that can also be a weak element in the overall approach of private schools where much emphasis is placed on basics and rigid structure. Up to the present, the law has not provided much help. Most states have some sort of gifted programs. All states have Gifted and Talented Consultants in their state education agencies (a list is available—see Resource List). The federal government has authorized the funding of some special pilot projects that may be applied for by the states.

No school district in the United States is compelled by federal law to provide any special education for the gifted child. As a consequence, at least one-third of known gifted children in our country receive no special instruction beyond what the regular classroom teacher may be able to provide. Who knows how many more children are out there still unidentified because their teachers and parents are unaware of their potential and/or what can be done to develop it.

If your school district has gifted programs in operation, look at them carefully before enrolling your child. Here are a few key questions to ask about the program:

1. Do district personnel have a strong belief in and commitment to gifted education? Look at the budget and see where the money is allocated. Ask why so little goes to gifted education. The reason may have more to do with state restrictions than local commitment, but find out. Talk with district coordinators for gifted and talented programs and find out how much backing they receive from the school board and the district superintendent. Ask what you can do to alleviate financial and priority imbalances. Let your state legislators know of your concern for increased funding for gifted education.

2. Does your district have adequately trained teachers for teaching gifted classes? Some school districts that would never consider assigning a teacher to a class of handicapped children without special training may pawn off the gifted program onto any teacher who is available or, worse yet, leave it in the hands of untrained volunteers. Several national organizations provide training for teachers of the gifted, but the idea has been a bit slow catching on.

3. Are identification processes up-to-date and administered fairly? Until recent years, gifted student identification was based almost entirely on IQ test scores. The newer federal definition of giftedness referred to earlier includes several other criteria for judgment that do not show up on those tests. A number of other tests are now available to help determine giftedness. One that is widely used is called SOI (Structure of Intellect). It measures many different kinds of intelligence besides the verbal, academic kind measured by IQ tests—things such as nonverbal, mechanical, and logical aptitudes (see Resource List for more information).

Some school districts, however, still rely largely on IQ scores. There are logical reasons for that. IQ testing is done in groups and requires less time and personnel than the individualized testing involved in other types of tests. It is also much simpler to assess a child's giftedness if the decision can be based solely on one or two test scores. It is usually true that a child who is gifted in other than academic areas will score higher than average on IQ tests as well. Some students, especially from foreign-born and culturally deprived homes may lack the foundation to allow the IQ test to accurately indicate their ability levels. Others, while having higher than normal IQ's, may fall one or two points below the established gifted level. If those children show particularly strong aptitude in other areas, they probably need the extra help and encouragement of a gifted program. Such tests as the SOI help to identify levels of aptitude in all the different kinds of intelligence. Knowing that allows a parent or an educator to plan an individualized educational plan for the child that will give special help in his weak areas and encouragement in the stronger ones.

4. Are the gifted children that are placed in a special school separated from the average students? That is usually not the wisest approach. No child is ever going to live in a world of all gifted people. Therefore, he should not get his education in such an artificial environment. If he is to become a leader of his generation, he needs to mix with those who will one day be his followers. He needs those contacts to constantly remind him of the many ways in which he is, after all, quite a common person. He will need help to keep from developing an elitist attitude that says, "I'm better than all the rest of those dumb kids!" Also, for some children, those intellectually segregated schools create too much pressure. Emotionally, the child cannot always handle the challenges of such a situation.

Usually it is best for a child to be in a regular classroom with a teacher who gives him extra attention and challenges him with extra work and responsibilities. He may become a part of a "pull-out" program where gifted students spend a part of each day or week in accelerated learning classes. It is seldom wise to allow a child to skip a grade, but the possibility should not be completely ruled out.

Some children seem to perform better when put in a class with all gifted children. They are forced to compete with peers who are equal or beyond them in ability. Even that kind of an arrangement generally works best when one or two special classes are located on a campus of mostly average level classes.

5. Do the gifted programs provide significant learning experiences for the children, or are they just fun and "artsy" games? One teacher complained that, in her school, gifted children were taken out of regular classes to make pottery and paint pictures. She could not see that as a significant substitute for classroom instruction. Such situations violate the intent of any gifted legislation that exists. State and/or federal programs are required to integrate enrichment cur-

riculum with classroom work so that those programs actually challenge the gifted student to set his sights a little higher and fully develop his special potential.

6. How much voice do parents have in approving and/or planning a gifted child's curriculum? When I asked one district Gifted and Talented Coordinator whether the writing of Individualized Education Plans was being done for gifted students as it now is for handicapped, she replied: "It's coming!" In much of the literature I have read from the various organizations that support gifted education, I have seen the initials *IEP*.

Parent involvement is essential for the success of gifted and talented education. Maybe your insistence will be the needed impetus for starting a program in your school. If your district has no such facilities, find out why. Offer your assistance, request a program, get yourself appointed to a district curriculum planning committee. Do everything you can to insure the establishment of a gifted and talented program in your school district. Before you begin writing senators and representatives at the state and federal levels about legislated gifted programs, however, take a look at the current handicapped legislation and ask yourself whether you really want all the same kinds of accompanying problems that such legislation brings.

Some parents have also banded together and formed extracurricular gifted and talented community groups for children. We have one in our county. Established by cooperating parents and educators, the organization provides seminars and unique field trip experiences for students in areas that public schools are unable to cover. Volunteer resource people who lead those seminars include teachers, doctors, engineers, artists, and many others. Perhaps you can help start such a group. It should never take the place of gifted and talented education in the school curriculum, however.

What is the function of the home in the life and education of a gifted or talented child? Our function as parents is basic. Here we establish attitudes of self-acceptance, enthusiasm for education, and willingness to voluntarily tackle the tougher challenges of life. A parent's responsibilities to the gifted and talented child are essentially these:

1. Accept him as a child. He should not be given preferential treatment or set on a pedestal. He should not be denied opportunities to go to parties, hike, swim, or "goof off" with other normal children of his age group. Let him lead a normal life. He is not some museum

relic for display. Do not use him as a standard by which you judge his siblings. It may be very important for you to warn the teachers of your average children that they are not to be compared with the gifted child in the family. Most teachers are already aware of this. But many will compare your children without even realizing it unless you call it to their attention. I know, because I have had to deal with that.

Just because your child may be a violinist is no reason why you need to make him give up playing ball for fear he might injure his fingers. He needs to be taught commonsense protection of his physical members needed for the exercise of his gifts. If he happens to be a clumsy person, he may have to limit some activities. To try to eliminate all the risks from his life is unrealistic and unhealthy for his attitude toward trying things. Part of being gifted is usually the drive to do new things and experiment with the rich smorgasbord that life offers to a growing child.

2. Encourage and support your child without pushing him. We do that mainly in three ways:

a) Expose the child to as many activities as possible. "Perhaps the most effective way to find the creative potentialities of children is to put them in an environment which encourages them to behave creatively."[9]

b) Appreciate the child for who he is and what he does and let him know it. Praise does wonders. It often serves as the shower that revives the wilting, yet exquisite, daisy.

c) Stimulate the child to try new things. Provide him with a wide range of physical activities—hikes, sports, bicycle riding, and the like. Resist the temptation to solve all his problems for him. Let him handle as many as he can on his own. Furnish him with games, toys, mechanical projects, great literature, challenging projects of all sorts that fall into his areas of giftedness and interest. Practice the art of stimulating conversation at mealtimes. One gifted child said of his home: "Usually . . . we tried to wait for the last person to arrive home for dinner, and [one] night was off limits for going out. Meals became an important time for sharing."[10]

3. If your child is a nonachiever, find out why. Gifted children fail to perform for a multitude of reasons. "Patterns of underachievement are established early."[11] If you have that problem, carry on a careful and prayerful search until you find the key. Is he bored? Under-challenged? Jealous of your attention? Distressed by conflict

in the home? Unwilling to be a peacock because the life of a sparrow looks like a lot more fun and less trouble? Are your attitudes right? What about school teachers? Peers?

4. Teach the gifted and talented child the biblical principles of equality before God and stewardship of gifts. All persons are gifted in some way. The most average person in the world may be gifted to use a dust mop and broom. Ability to perform menial tasks cheerfully without boredom and to the glory of God is a rare gift.

We Christians have in our Bibles the most priceless teaching tool for dealing with that need. Here we learn that the Christian community is like a body where each member has equal value and a unique function. Study 1 Corinthians 12 and share its truth with *all* your children—the gifted, the ordinary, and the handicapped. Giftedness in the Body of Christ never means increased worth. The mouth is no more important than the little toenail. Because the one is more obvious, he has a greater responsibility, however, to properly represent the interests of the entire body. Each person in your home has been given a specific gift or, more likely a combination of gifts. With his gifts he also receives the responsibilities of using them for the proper functioning of the Body and for the purpose of honoring both his family and Jesus Christ, who gifted him. The more outstanding his gifts, the greater the responsibility to God, his family, and to all mankind.

Children are not too immature to learn those principles. If we begin early to teach them and to model them in our everyday living, our children will be extraordinarily gifted children indeed.

NOTES

1. Herbert Kanigher, *Everyday Enrichment for Gifted Children at Home and School* (Los Angeles: Ventura County Superintendent of Schools, 1977), p. vi.
2. *The Challenge of the Gifted.* Handbook for the Mentally Gifted Minor Program of Fremont Union High School District, Sunnyvale, California, n.d., p. 5.
3. James J. Gallagher and Patricia Weiss, *The Education of Gifted and Talented Students: A History and Prospectus* (Washington, D.C.: Council for Basic Education, 1979, p. 1.
4. "Handicapped: the Unserved," *NETWORK* (Columbia, Maryland: NCCE, April 1979), p. 7.
5. Harold Lyon, cited in *The Challenge of the Gifted*, p. 29.

6. "Parents of Gifted and Talented Children," Fact sheet (Reston, Virginia: Council for Exceptional Children, 1978), p. 1.
7. Ibid.
8. Eric Johnson, *Teaching School: Points Picked Up* (Boston: Nat'l Ass'n of Independent Schools, 1979), cited in *Gifted Children's Newsletter,* May 1980, p. 5.
9. Hoppock, cited in *The Challenge of the Gifted,* p. 13.
10. American Association for Gifted Children, *On Being Gifted* (New York: Walker, 1978), p. 53.
11. Gallagher and Weiss, p. 10.

16

ARMING FOR THE FUTURE

*To teach someone is to change someone. . . . Putting aside
the whims and fancies and ignorance of childhood, all the
while replacing them with the wisdom, the understandings,
the insights and values of a rich biblical perspective.*[1]

Norman DeJong

LIKE THE WORK OF A HOUSEWIFE, the education of the next generation is never done. We spend a quarter of a century guiding, hover-
ing over, modeling, praying over, and supervising each child God
gives to us. Finally, the day comes when we have paid the last
college tuition fees. We sit teary-eyed through the wind and hot sun
or the school auditorium mustiness of our final college commencement. The ceremonies over, we give our eager graduate a special,
one-of-a-kind hug. With that hug, we pass on to him the commission
we have been fulfilling all those years—the primary responsibility for
the future of education.

That is one of the most valuable legacies we bequeath to the young
adults that emerge from those wiggly, little boy and girl cocoons that
we have so carefully nourished. Inherent in that legacy are the
problems we have faced but could not totally resolve, along with a
host of new challenges and constantly changing resources. Also inherent in the legacy are the attitudes we have modeled and taught
through our children's nestling years. Passing on the responsibility
begins way back on day one, when we first started the education
process.

How then can we, as parents, adequately prepare our children to
live up to the commission we give to them on commencement day?
How can we continue to be involved with the future of education?

Can we assume any responsibilities now that we are no longer those prime consumers of education called "Johnny's parents"?

First, let us look at how we can prepare our children for their big job. That is something we do both consciously and unconsciously. By conscious effort we can encourage them to consider careers in education. Preparing to be a schoolteacher is not too popular an idea in our time. Comparatively low salaries, heavy work loads, a poor job market, increasing violence, and government regulation discourage many young people. Our newspapers run headlines like these on the public opinion pages: *Smartest Students Are Too Smart to Go into Underpaid, Overworked Teaching Jobs; Educators Made into Scapegoats for Society's Problems.*

Many areas of our country are seeing massive teacher layoffs and program cutbacks caused by declining enrollments and slashed budgets. Educational careers offer unstable prospects in terms of job security. Teachers are being forced, either by low pay or by job cuts, to go into the world of industry in search of a livelihood. In such a climate, a young person with a teaching aptitude and interest needs all the encouragement we can give him.

When the outlook is so gloomy, why should we urge a child to pray and prepare for a career in education? Pat Patchen, executive secretary for the National Educators Fellowship, suggests one good reason: "The need for Christians in the teaching profession has never been more urgent. As others are being advised to turn from the profession, why not urge Christian youth to enter it in a greater way than ever before? . . . The future may call for fewer teachers, but it will never cease to call for teachers. And it will always call for the best."[2]

The phenomenal growth of Christian day schools has created a totally different situation for Christian teachers. Many missionary organizations need teachers to teach missionary children around the world. The pay is often quite a bit lower in Christian schools and in some new private schools. If God has gifted a child to be a teacher, his parents can help him to see that he has a stewardship responsibility to teach, in some capacity. One of the most important things we can do for such children is to encourage them to consecrate their abilities to God and to let Him set their standard of living, as they are obedient to His leading.

Career education and encouragement are, at least in part, a matter of exposure. A friend of mine is married to a college education professor. A couple of years ago they took their family to South America for a short-term missionary project that became an experience in career exposure for their three girls. The father taught missionary teachers as a part of a special service program. You and I may not be able to do that, but we can get acquainted with Christian educators and invite them to our homes where they can interact with our children. We can encourage our children to pay special attention to how certain exemplary teachers teach and, particularly, how Christian teachers live out their faith.

Not only can we consciously encourage our children to consider educational careers, the truth of the matter is that we all unconsciously either encourage or discourage them by our day-to-day attitudes toward education and our level of involvement in it.

Our positive attitudes accomplish much in making present-day education effective in the lives of our children. In addition, our expressions of hope for the future, based on confidence in the God whom we honor as Commander-in-Chief of the Army for Quality Schools, will prove amazingly contagious. If we, as parents, continue to take adult education courses, or pursue active research on topics that interest us, or lead our children into independent excursions into the wonder-world of learning, those things all contribute to building the kind of positive attitudes that the next generation will need to make education work. My husband and I have always found great satisfaction in sharing learning projects with our children. We still enjoy a lot of that satisfaction now that they are grown. Relationships based on growing and learning meet a need so deep that we and our children can hardly go on to maturity without them.

How we arrange our priorities will also be contagious. A teacher complained to me that many school committees failed to attract Christian parents because their meetings were scheduled on church prayer meeting nights. "Few Christian parents will give up a church meeting in order to serve in their community," she said. One church we belonged to solved that problem by changing the church mid-week service to a different night in order to free parents for Wednesday night school meetings. In one of the newer basics schools in our area, Christian parents requested that meetings be held on nights other than Wednesday. Because of the commitment and quantity of church parents involved in that school, their request was granted. The pastor of another church told me that when his children were young, his wife had missed prayer meeting more than once in order to attend a school function. On the other side of the priority picture, there will be times when the church function must come first. That too becomes a learning experience for the child in setting his priorities for life.

My involvement for my children's education sets an important pattern for them to establish some expectations of parents in their generation. When our children become educators, they will have an idea what a good parent/teacher team can mean in the education of a child.

One teacher told me that a key problem in education today is the lack of parent/teacher communication and cooperation. She claims that many teachers do not feel secure about their professional image in the eyes of parents. At the same time, parents fear the teachers and have no idea how to break the ice in their relationship. Most parents have contact with a teacher only when there is trouble. That sort of problem-based relationship building is far from healthy. It nurtures an attitude of personal irresponsibility, buck-passing, and mutual suspicion that leads to negative bitterness and panic.

Contrary to that pattern, if we model for our children a positive, cooperative relationship between parents and teachers, they will become the kind of teachers who know how to approach parents and/or the kind of parents who have no fear of approaching teachers.

Our investment in the future of education is not restricted, however, to preparing our children to assume our parent commission or to embark on educational careers. No law says that when we cease to be "Classroom Johnny's Parents," we must abdicate all involvement and stop playing guardian. On the contrary, when our children are grown and gone from home, many of us have increased time to give to volunteer or political education projects. Some of us mothers may feel freer to take on paid positions at that time in our lives. Now, however, our motivation is tested in new ways. Obviously, we will no longer work to insure our own children's education. Perhaps our grandchildren will not even benefit from what we do in our communities. We must look, instead, for wider motivations—service to our communities and to our God.

One couple in Texas followed the volunteer route as they put six children through school. They were active in PTA, tutoring, textbook selection, fund-raising, sports, and field trips. Today they continue to offer the same volunteer services. It has become a vital part of their lives and a continued ministry to their community.

Our continued involvement in education will not necessarily be much different in nature from what we have done all along. Now we can concentrate more than ever on bringing into focus the following:

1. At every level of involvement, we need to set high standards. That means excellence in academics, in discipline, in teacher concern, and in administration.

2. It is imperative to keep a close check on future trends as they develop. We must read about pending legislation, new theories and methods, community demands, and experiments in other places. Then we can be vocal about our reactions.

3. We should encourage Christians we know to pray for education and educators. Perhaps you will find a ministry like one Southern California couple. They have formed a group of prayer warriors who pray for individual schools in their community. They even talk with principals and ask for specific requests. At least you can obtain requests from teachers and take them to prayer meetings of your church or your neighborhood, or wherever two or three gather in His name to pray.

4. We need to ask God to give us compassionate hearts. When looking at the immense, apparently insoluble, problems of modern education, it is so easy to become harshly critical of those who seem to be to blame for the mess we are in. We cannot afford to be like the man who told his pastor, "I want you to know that God has given me the spiritual gift of criticism." Exhortation, perhaps, but nowhere in Scripture does God ever say that criticism is one of the gifts of the Spirit.

To me, it is tremendously significant that the same man who wrote, "Put on the whole armour of God" (Ephesians 6:11), and, "Fight the good fight of faith" (1 Timothy 6:12), also wrote: "And we urge you brethren, admonish the unruly, encourage the fainthearted, help the weak, *be patient with all men*" (1 Thessalonians 5:14, NASB, italics added).

The "castle on the hill" casts its shadow across all our lives. The shadow runs straight down the road into our future. That can be very bad, or it can be very good. Much of the choice is up to you and me, parents and regiment captains in the vigorous Army for Quality Schools.

No matter where we fight, we all hear rumors. In spite of what we hear, we need to know that the majority of America's educators still place the home at the top of the list in responsibility for child nurture, development, and education.

"Parents have the ultimate responsibility for the upbringing of their children. . . . The school's authority ends when it infringes on this parental right," said former US Commissioner of Education, T. H. Bell.[3]

A schoolteacher from Arizona told me: "Parents in both secular and Christian schools are going to have to come to grips with the fact that *they* have to assume the responsibility for the education of their children." Another teacher, from Chicago's inner city, said, "Parents should take back from the state the responsibilities for their children's education."

In a 1972 decision (*Wisconsin* v. *Yoder*), a federal court issued the following statement:

"The primary role of the parents in the upbringing of their children is now established beyond debate as an enduring American tradition."[4]

What are we waiting for? Let us take our places at the head of our regiments and get on with the battle at hand!

NOTES

1. Norman DeJong, *Philosophy of Education: A Christian Approach* (Nutley, N.J.: Presbyterian and Reformed, 1977), p. 25.
2. Pat Patchen, *Vision* (NEF [National Educators Fellowship] magazine), August/September, 1973, p. 9.
3. From interview with Mrs. George W. Abrigg, Jr. "An Insidious Monopoly," *Manion Forum*, South Bend, Ind., April 20, 27, and May 4, 1975, p. 4.
4. David Schimmel and Louis Fischer, *The Rights of Parents in the Education of Their Children* (Columbia, Maryland: NCCE, 1977).

17

RESOURCE LIST

*I value highly the facts and philosophies and opinions I
learned about in school, but even more useful is the knowledge of where to find out what I don't know.*[1]

Max Gunther

THIS BOOK IS A BASIC TRAINING MANUAL, a first step in the process of
learning about education. I trust that in its brief chapters you have
got a feel for the scope and the nature of the battle you face. I
hope you have also become excited about taking your place in the
Army for Quality Schools. As you go out to battle, however, you will
need more weapons and more training in the strategies especially
suited to your battlefield. In fact, as long as you are in the "army,"
you will continue to need to read and train, always sharpening your
skills as an effective soldier, or nurse, or commissary stock boy.

Toward this end, I want to share with you some of the resources
that I have found helpful over the years. I have read or had dealings
with most of the books, magazines, newsletters, and organizations.
Some I have not felt qualified to evaluate, so I have received evaluations from experts who know enough to give a fair critique.

My list is in no way exhaustive. The volume of materials on the
subject of education is unbelievably huge. Obviously, I could not
even read all that I could find. Further, I have read many things
that I will not recommend to you for a number of reasons.

In the next few pages, I present to you a glimpse into my book-
shelves and the file folder marked "Resources." I also urge you to
build your own resource file. Search your library, current magazines,
bookstores (new and secondhand), and even garage sales. Get ideas
from other parents and educators, especially for help with specific

subjects. Follow up on the leads you find in magazines and books. Send for sample copies, free materials, catalogs and bibliographies. If you cannot afford to buy some of the books, request your public library to purchase them. Check your local school and district libraries.

Before I give you my personal notes of recommendation, I want to share with you some warnings and guidelines as you go out and start digging up more materials for yourself. We can never believe or act upon everything we read. The points of view are often contradictory, for education is a highly controversial topic. Certainly not all we read will agree with our philosophy of life or of education. We must learn to be discerning.

First, a few warnings. As we read through the materials we find, we need to watch for four things:

1. *Viewpoint of the authors or organization leaders.* Are they prejudiced in any way (e.g., anti-public or anti-Christian education)? Do they insist that there is only one solution to any one educational dilemma? Do they allow for Spirit-directed individualized creative problem-solving? Is their philosophy of life based on atheistic humanism or is it biblical? I have one book on my shelf that I picked up in a secondhand store. Quickly previewing it, I discovered a chapter on values where the authors revealed a moral philosophy that promotes situation ethics and relative values. Everything that I have since read in that book, I have read with that in mind. Consequently, I have rejected those ideas that I feel reflect a morally ambivalent point of view.

2. *Tone of the writing.* Does the material present a sensible examination of the issues and encourage the reader to think through all the angles before arriving at a conclusion? Or is it an impassioned tract, depending upon the use of scare tactics to motivate the reader to go out and start swinging a sword? I do not discount the unselfish and concerned motives that prompt such "prophets of doom," but I do know the terrible depression and hopelessness that such materials can inspire. One item I read was even entitled "Read It and Weep." The assumption is that if we weep, we will naturally do something about the situation. One man I interviewed reminded me that unfortunately many people are never aroused to do anything unless they are whipped into a panic. As we have discussed in the earlier chapters of this book, that sort of thing is dangerous. Panicky people

rarely accomplish divine purposes or do the right thing and often do much harm instead.

3. *Fairness.* Does the material present facts on all sides of an issue? Does it give shocking examples and leave the reader with the impression that those conditions exist everywhere? Does it encourage us to adopt a witch-hunting mentality, to question every motive, mistrust every innovation, and view every educator and textbook with suspicion?

As I researched this book, the thing that most disturbed me was the volume of books and newsletters that presented only the negative side of our educational system. They ignored all the good things that are happening. Consistently they refused to simply report situations and current problems. Into every report they seemed duty-bound to inject some strong doses of editorial venom, designed to arouse the reader's anger. More than once I laid a book or magazine aside because the author made me feel that everything was wrong with every school. I knew better and refused to go on reading.

4. *Constructiveness.* Is the author interested only in giving you a vivid exposé of the evil? Does he offer some constructive, tested, and proved suggestions? When I read specific, helpful suggestions for parents, I know that there is hope, if I will just do my part in the battlefield of God's choice for me. Some newsletters, in their eagerness to share all the ideas they can find, pass on addresses, stories, and suggestions to their readers without first checking into them and evaluating them for themselves. For that reason, when I follow up an address lead from a newsletter, I always send for sample copies of publications rather than subscribing sight unseen. In the process, I have found some things that never should have been recommended. Further, I have refused to buy some expensive books that might be quite helpful, simply because I cannot look at them before buying.

Finally, what do we do with the materials we decide to read?

1. Evaluate them according to the guidelines given above. Check what the reading of a book does to your blood pressure. Does it poison your thinking about an educator or a school system? What does it do to your confidence in God? Can you sort out the good from the bad in the material as you read it? If not, discard it.

2. Compare reports. Check on the accuracy of statistics and analyses of events and trends. Remember the value of there being more than one witness. Take time to think a matter through and let

your blood cool before you grab your sword. Talk with other parents, teachers, or Christian education specialists whose opinions you trust.

3. Remember that there is no one right answer for every child or every recurrence of a common problem. Do not let anybody tell you that there is.

4. Pray before you do anything. God is, after all, the Commander in Chief. Nothing has to be done with such urgency that it cannot await His orders.

5. Do what you can do, as God tells you to do it. Encourage others to do their part. Pray a lot about everything that needs to be done. And expect God to do great things in your school situation!

In the Resource List that follows, you will find a variety of books, magazine articles, organizations, and periodicals. They are categorized according to the subject headings of chapters in this book. For most items listed, a fee will be charged. I have not listed prices, as they change rapidly. Always ask about the fee when requesting information or materials. In the case of organizations that may not ask a set fee, I suggest that you make a donation if you are pleased with the organization.

NOTE

1. Max Gunther, *Writing and Selling a Nonfiction Book* (Boston: The Writer, 1973), p. 44.

RESOURCES

GENERAL

Barclay, William. *Educational Ideals in the Ancient World.* Grand Rapids: Baker, 1959. Excellent background for origins of Western education. Of special interest are chapters on education in Hebrew history and early church.

Cordasco, Francesco. *A Brief History of Education.* Totowa, N.J.: Littlefield, Adams, 1970. One of many books giving survey of history of education. Helpful outline of dates, persons, trends, and statistics.

Council for Basic Education, 725 Fifteenth St., NW, Washington, D.C. 20005. Organization that supports teachers and parents in efforts to strengthen mastery of basic school subjects. Dues-paying members receive monthly 20-page bulletins of news and ideas in basic education, plus occasional papers printed throughout the year. Written primarily for educators, materials are a bit technical but helpful to parents. All materials printed by CBE in list below available from above address.

McGraw, Onalee, ed., *Education Update.* Published periodically by the Heritage Foundation, 513 C St. NE, Washington, D.C. 20002. Usually exposé in nature, though they offer some helpful suggestions and names and addresses of active parent groups and new books on education. Also print booklets occasionally. Write for more information.

National Committee for Citizens in Education, Suite 410, Wilde Lake Village Green, Columbia, MD 21044. Highly recommended organization serving as liaison between school system and parents. Membership includes subscription to *NETWORK* (monthly newspaper about parent concerns) and newly-published booklets of most practical nature. NCCE also helps parents organize in local groups to promote their concerns. Everything I have seen from this organization is excellent and helpful. All materials printed by NCCE in list below available from address above.

National Educator's Fellowship, Box 243, S. Pasadena, CA 91030. National organization of Christian professional educators who serve in both public and private schools. Provides local fellowship groups, literature, a magazine, annual national convention—all designed to inspire, inform, counsel, and encourage Christian educators. Good source of information for parents as well.

CHAPTER 2

Alexander, John W. *Education: A Christian View.* Downers Grove, Ill.: Inter-Varsity, 1978. Excellent treatment of purposes, mistakes, and suggestions for education from Christian perspective. Obtain free by writing Inter-Varsity Press, Box F, Downers Grove, IL 60515.

CHAPTER 4

Frisbie, Richard, and Frisbie, Margaret, *The Do-It-Yourself Parent.* New York: Sheed and Ward, 1963. Detailed, practical ideas for helping educate children at home in preparation for school. Book is old, however. Written from obvious Catholic slant.

McGraw, Onalee. *Secular Humanism and the Schools: The Issue Whose Time Has Come.* Washington, D.C.: Heritage Foundation, 1976. Clear picture of what secular humanism is, how it is promoted in school systems, and what legally can be done to stop it.

Student Action for Christ, P.O. Box 1008, Herrin, IL 62948. Work to prepare Christian high school students to face godlessness on campus, challenge unbiblical teachings, and witness to friends and teachers. Publish high school newspaper for campus distribution, newspaper for parents and educators, and book for students on evidence for the integrity and reliability of the Bible. Operate some weekend seminars in churches to train lay people to deal with public school problems. Maintain staff of qualified speakers who speak in classrooms on topics such as "Science, Evolution, and Creation," "Where Is History Going?" and the like. Information available upon request by telephone or writing (address requests to Randy Rodden).

CHAPTER 5

"Academic Freedom and the Alternative School" and "More About Basic Alternative Schools" Newsletters 36 and 37. Available from L.I.T.E., 6122 North 8th Ave., Phoenix, AZ 85013. Helpful look at

history, rationale behind, and specific suggestions for how to start
basic schools.

Basic Education Leadership Conference, 422 S. Murphy Ave. #2,
Sunnyvale, CA 94086. Organization that assists individuals and
groups in establishing basic schools. Also provides materials, consulting services, conferences, and training for all involved or interested in basic schools education.

Calvert School, Tuscany Road, Baltimore, MD 21210. Leading correspondence school in this country for nearly 100 years. Used by
missionaries, families involved in traveling occupations, and those
teaching their own children at home.

Christian School Networks. Several exist, and here are the three
major ones:

American Association of Christian Schools (AACS) 1017 N.
School St., Normal, IL 61761. Nearly 900 member schools, representing fundamentalist church groups.

The Association of Christian Schools International (ACSI), P.O.
Box 4097, Whittier, CA 90607. Over 1,000 schools in this organization. Composed of mostly mainline evangelical churches.

Christian Schools International (CSI), 3350, E. Paris Ave., SE,
Grand Rapids, MI 49508. Just under 400 member schools, mostly
among Reformed churches.

Love, Robert. *How to Start Your Own School.* Ottawa, Ill.: Green
Hill Pub., 1973. Story of beginning of independent, community-
founded and financed school in Wichita, Kansas. Includes specific
advice on how to start your own school. Attitude is very negative
toward public education, but advice is valuable. Order directly
from Green Hill Publishers, Box 738, Ottawa, IL 61350.

Myers, Henry S., Jr. *Fundamentally Speaking.* San Francisco: Strawberry Hill, 1977. Story of how one basic school started. Includes
valuable suggestions for others who want to start basic schools.

"Your Child and the Back to Basics Movement," *Better Homes and
Gardens,* April 1979, pp. 15-30. Excellent article summarizing the
reasons for basic schools, their philosophy, operation, problems,
and suggestions for starting them.

CHAPTER 6

"How Effective Are Your Schools? A Checklist for Citizens." Developed by Council for Basic Education; helps you evaluate qual-

ity of your school in terms of factors that matter for learning. Deals with areas of leadership, basic subjects, academic programs, teachers' values, discipline, and support from parents and community.

CHAPTER 7

Annual Education Checkup. Card produced by NCCE as a guide to parent-teacher conferences. Includes questions to ask and hints about conference follow-up, records review, action, and appeals. Available in English and Spanish.

Dyer, Henry S. *Parents Can Understand Testing.* Columbia, Md.: 1980. NCCE. Complete coverage of subject. Answers such questions as: Why do schools give tests? How reliable are different kinds of tests? What are the problems with testing and scores? What questions should I ask about the tests my child takes? Includes helpful chart of state testing requirements, glossary of testing terms, and bibliography for further study. Excellent source.

The Home and School Institute, 1707 H St., NW, Washington, D.C. 20006. Works through seminars, workshops, and written materials to help home and school work together. Publishes a book of "home learning recipes" that outlines activities parents can do with children in everyday life to help with math and reading concepts. Teachers and parents evaluating them for me thought they were good, but elementary—a good starting point.

Mantz, Barbara. "How to Help Your Kids in School," *Better Homes and Gardens,* November 1977, pp. 14-18. Explains current trend to make education a parent/teacher partnership project, showing how parents can help this happen.

Parent's Guide to Understanding Tests. Available free upon request, with inclusion of a self-addressed stamped envelope, from Frank W. Snyder, Editorial Director, CTB/McGraw Hill, Del Monte Research Park, Monterey, CA 93940. Small booklet explaining kinds of tests given to our children and suggesting how we can use test scores to plan and assist the child with educational progress and goals.

Weiss, Benjamin. *Great Thoughts.* Pasadena: National Educators Fellowship, 1971. Teaching packet of flash cards and explanatory booklet, using quotations from the Bible and great men in history. Effective for introducing great thoughts for discussion. Designed for teachers' use, but also useful in the home. Available from NEF.

CHAPTER 8

Barton, Jon T. "Teaching the Bible in Public Schools." *Christianity Today,* 7 September 1979, pp. 19-22. Excellent interview article, explaining legal rights of teachers to teach Bible in public schools.

Hall, Christopher. *The Christian Teacher and the Law.* Oak Park, Ill.: Christian Legal Society, 1975. Helpful analysis of (1) legal rights and opportunities of teachers in public schools and (2) biblical standards for motivation and godly perspective on Christian liberty. This and other materials (legal memoranda, briefs, law review articles applying to religious liberty in education) available from Center for Law and Religious Freedom, P.O. Box 2069, Oak Park, IL 60303.

Kappelman, Murray, and Ackerman, Paul. *Between Parent and School.* New York: Dial/James Wade, 1977. Chapters 1, 22, and 25 present legal rights and responsibilities of parents and educators, focusing especially on needs of handicapped students. Shows parents of handicapped how to serve as their children's advocate in getting the education available by law.

Legal information (Christmas programs). From National Educators Fellowship. You can order a copy of Memorandum Opinion of US District Court, Rapid City, South Dakota, on legality of Christmas programs in public schools. Useful documentary evidence for legal precedence for such issues in your school or district.

Panoch, James V., and Barr, David L. *Religion Goes to School.* New York: Harper & Row, 1968. Explains rationale and content of anti-prayer-and-Bible-reading amendment (see Appendix 5) and how that affects religious instruction in public classrooms. Includes lengthy list of materials available for religious instruction in classrooms.

"Parents Rights Card." Published and distributed by NCCE. Wallet-sized card listing twenty-one rights you may have as parents of children in public schools. Indicates in which states each right was granted, as of November 1977. Available in both Spanish and English.

Schimmel, David, and Fischer, Louis. *The Rights of Parents in the Education of Their Children.* Columbia, Md.: NCCE, 1977. Detailed explanation of all legal rights of parents and students. Written by two lawyers who are also professors of education, it is a comprehensive work, readable by average parent, valuable as an aid to working knowledgeably with our children's educators.

CHAPTER 9

Esmay, Judith. *Collective Bargaining and Teacher Strikes*. Columbia, Md.: NCCE, 1978. Explains collective bargaining in education and tells you how to get involved in the process (1) before bargaining begins, (2) during bargaining, (3) after negotiations, and (4) in event of a strike. Contains sample teacher's contract, table of state regulations concerning collective bargaining, glossary of terms, bibliography, and checklist of materials needed to begin work with collective bargaining process.

Marburger, Carl. *Who Controls the Schools?* Columbia, Md.: NCCE, 1978. One of the most helpful books I found. Every parent should have it. Surveys for average parent the roles of all sorts of educators and governmental agencies, helps you to identify where real power lies in your public education system, and gives excellent advice on parent advisory groups. Includes list (with names and addresses) of several hundred such groups functioning as members of NCCE's Parent's Network.

Parents Organizing to Improve Schools. Columbia, Md.: NCCE, 1976. I have not read this, but believe it is recommendable. Step-by-step guide to organizing and running parent groups in schools and involving parents in a lasting way. Available in both English and Spanish.

Parents Who Care. Gunn Senior High School, 780 Arastradero Road, Palo Alto, CA 94304. Rapidly growing organization involving parents in the control of drugs, vandalism, and so on. For story of beginnings of this movement, request booklet "Parents, Pot and Peers" from National Clearinghouse for Drug Abuse Information, Room 10A56, Parklawn Building, 5600 Fishers Lane, Rockville, MD 20857. One copy free. For more information about the organization and how you can start one in your area, use address above.

Warren, Rita. *Mom, They Won't Let Us Pray*. Waco, Tex.: Word, 1975. Colorful story of immigrant mother's reaction to Bible reading and prayer ammendment. Tells how she put a statute on books of Massachusetts, allowing moment of silent meditation in classrooms.

You, the Schools, and Collective Bargaining. A handbook for California citizens, written by and available from Information Project on Educational Negotiations (IPEN), 810 Miranda Green, Palo Alto, CA 94306. Inexpensive. Clear, concise guidelines for citizens.

Includes glossary, list of resources, and sample displays of kinds of documents you will encounter in your search for facts. Also publishes periodic newsletter and offers specialized assistance to all who call or write about their specific problems with contract negotiations, strikes, and so on.

CHAPTER 10

Dersh, Rhoda. *School Budget: It's Your Money—It's Your Business.* Columbia, Md.: NCCE, 1979. Explains in truly readable style what a school budget is and how to understand, evaluate, change, and gain some input in budget planning process. Covers every area of subject in great detail. Highly recommended by outstanding organizations and educators around the country.

CHAPTER 11

America's Future, Inc., 542 Main Street, New Rochelle, NY 10801. Organization that provides evaluations of high school textbooks in history, civics, sociology, and economics and furnishes them to high schools all over the country, free of charge, upon request. Write for information and sample evaluations and lists of books that they have reviewed.

Black, Hillel. *The American Schoolbook.* New York: William Morrow, 1967. Instructive book on how textbooks are planned and written. Provides helpful insights into the textbook industry that parents need to understand.

Citizens for Scientific Creation, Santa Clara County, P.O. Box 164, Saratoga, CA 95070. Nancy Stake organization, whose story appears in chapter 11 of this book. Offers pamphlets on scientific creation and evolution and specific assistance to parents wanting to get creation education into their schools.

Creation Science Research Center, P.O. Box 23195, San Diego, CA 92123. Write for *Action Manual,* 28-page packet of materials to help you get the teaching of scientific creationism into your school. Also contains important evaluations of currently used science textbooks.

Gabler, Mel, and Gabler, Norma. "A Parent's Guide to Textbook Review and Reform." Brief summary of parental involvement, along with address for Gablers, in order to receive further help and information. Good for distribution in groups. Available from Heritage Foundation, 513 C St., NE, Washington, D.C. 20002.

Hefley, James. *Are Textbooks Harming Your Children?* Milford, Mich.: Mott Media, 1979. Story of Mel and Norma Gabler's campaign to clean up textbooks of Texas and help parents to do the same around the country. Contains much helpful advice and inspiration.

Institute for Creation Research, 2716 Madison Ave., San Diego, CA 92116. Organization that publishes creationist materials for all ages, including outstanding books for children. Monthly mailing available—newsletter for the organization and technical papers on creationism topics.

Lorand, Rhoda L. "The Betrayal of Youth." 11-page exposé of problems with Planned Parenthood's sex education programs being used in many (though not all) public school systems. Read cautiously and do not panic. Use as a guideline to help you evaluate what programs exist in your school. Available from Heritage Foundation, 513 C St. NE, Washington, D.C. 20002.

CHAPTER 12

Campus Crusade for Christ has trained persons who give lectures on scientific, economic, and social/moral topics in high schools and colleges. Available in most areas where colleges or universities exist. For information, address them at Arrowhead Springs, San Bernardino, CA 92414.

CSB (Christian School Books), P.O. Box 155, Hubbard, OH 44425. Organization of volunteers who place Christian books in school libraries. Books are free to schools, already processed, and ready to place on shelves. Volunteers contact librarians, then raise funds from local churches to purchase books and place them. Write for information if you are interested in becoming a book volunteer.

Institute for Public Affairs Research, Inc. (IPAR), 516 SE Morrison, Suite 711, Portland, OR 97214. Nonprofit organization using volunteers for city-wide career education program. Write for packet of materials.

Music for Minors. P.O. Box 1143, Los Altos, CA 94022. Nonprofit, privately-funded organization that trains and places volunteer music instructors in classrooms. For information on how this works, write address above.

Ross, Dr. Hugh. Sierra Madre Congregational Church, 170 W. Sierra Madre Blvd., Sierra Madre, CA 91024. Brilliant astro-physicist who gives lectures in private and public schools on science, apologetics, archaeology, and economics, with biblical application. Available for engagements by invitation, providing that schedule allows and travel expenses are paid.

CHAPTER 13

"November 1976—The Changing of the Guard." Ten-page paper on how to function as a responsible, godly school board member. Request newsletter number 44 from L.I.T.E., 9340 W. Peoria Ave., Peoria, AZ 85345.

CHAPTER 14

Council for Exceptional Children, 1920 Association Drive, Reston, VA 22091. Organization highly recommended by many persons working with handicapped children. Write for information about materials and services available. Among others things, they have a clearinghouse of research information about handicapped children and their needs.

Fisher, Johanna. *A Parent's Guide To Learning Disabilities.* New York: Scribner's, 1978. I have only scanned this book, but it comes highly recommended. Includes practical helps, even on how to help prevent development of some learning disabilities.

Kappelman, Murray, and Ackerman, Paul. *Between Parent & School.* New York: Dial, 1977. Helpful analysis of kinds of assistance available for children with various kinds of handicaps. Also valuable information of legal nature.

Osman, Betty B. *Learning Disabilities: A Family Affair.* New York, Random House, 1979. A brief scanning indicates to me that this book would be helpful. Many organizations (national, state, and local) exist for families with specific handicap problems. In your search for the organization that can help and encourage you, begin by asking your child's special education teacher, counselor, or school district personnel. Other places where you can find names and addresses in your area:

    Telephone book
    City or county information services
    State Department of Rehabilitation (usually with local offices)
    State Department of Social Services
    State Department of Public Health

CHAPTER 15

American Association for Gifted Children, 15 Gramercy Park, New York, NY 10003. Will send price list of materials available upon request. I have found their paper, "Guideposts for Parents of Gifted Children," to be a helpful starting point.

Council for Exceptional Children, ERIC Clearinghouse on Handicapped and Gifted Children, 1920 Association Dr., Reston, VA 22091. Ask for gifted packet containing book lists, brochures describing their services, and fact sheet about giftedness.

Daly, Margaret. "Schools and the Gifted Child." *Better Homes and Gardens,* May 1979, pp. 19ff. Good overview of characteristics and problems of gifted children.

Gallagher, James J., and Weiss, Patricia. *The Education of Gifted and Talented Students: A History and Prospectus.* CBE Occasional Papers series. Washington, D.C.: Council for Basic Education, 1979. Excellent insights and perspectives for parents of gifted children, especially those who are underachievers, unidentified, and/or neglected by educational system.

Gifted Child Newsletter, 6185 Arapahoe St., P.O. Box 2581, Boulder, CO 80322. Send for sample copy (enclose $1.00). Attractive, practical, documented magazine for parents of gifted and talented students. Hints, information, and activities to use with your children.

Lyceum of the Monterey Peninsula, 24945 Valley Way, Carmel, CA 93921. Contact for information on starting a parent-organized program of enrichment seminars and experiences for gifted students.

National/State Leadership Training Institute for the Gifted and Talented, 316 W. Second St., Suite PH-C, Los Angeles, CA 90012. Write for catalog of materials, training opportunities, and information. Offers over twenty book titles dealing with all phases of gifted and talented education. Of special interest to parents is the "Parents Package" consisting of three books:

> *Parents Speak on Gifted and Talented Children.* Collection of six articles written by parents, dealing with rationale for gifted education, how to organize parent groups, and practical hints for home support. "This book is dynamite!" one parent told me.
>
> Delp, Jeanne L., and Martinson, Ruth A. *A Handbook for Parents of Gifted and Talented.* Recommended for both parents

and educators. Goes into more depth than *Parents Speak* and gives resources for parents to use at home.

Kanigher, Herbert. *Everyday Enrichment.* Intensely practical collection of specific educational activities you can share with your gifted child.

SOI Institute, 343 Richmond St., El Segundo, CA 90150. Private, non-profit, educational research corporation offering educational services to teachers and parents of gifted and talented students. Materials are based on the Structure of Intellect thesis that "all children have intelligence in varying degrees, *in various abilities."* SOI provides teacher and parent training, classroom aids, tests of both degree and kinds of native intelligence, individualized computer analyses of a child's strong and weak areas, individualized workbooks to help strengthen weak areas and develop strong ones, and career and vocational counseling. For more information, write above address.

CHAPTER 16

Gray, Dennis. *Minimum Competency Testing: Guidelines for Policymakers and Citizens.* CBE Occasional Papers series, 1980. Helpful for parents and community members involved in minimum competency testing planning. Explains what minimum competency is, examines its limitations, weighs the criticisms, shows how to plan for and utilize it to best advantage

Intercristo, Box 9323, Seattle, WA 98109. Organization helps Christian young people find employment and ministry around the world. Useful for your child in seeking Christian career guidance.

GLOSSARY

ACCELERATION. Process of allowing a child to progress more rapidly than his peers by means of grade skipping.

ACHIEVEMENT TEST. Measures child's academic achievement in given areas (usually reading, grammar, math, science, and social studies).

ACT. (*See* SAT).

ADMINISTRATOR. School principal or specialized administrative educator with ability to execute and manage school affairs.

ADVANCED PLACEMENT. Special classes offered to gifted children, preparing them for college and university. In some cases students take tests that will exempt them from certain college courses.

ADVISORY COMMITTEE OR COUNCIL. Group of parents, community members, and educators serving as advisors to school administration and faculty. Rarely has power to take action.

APTITUDE TEST. Measures a child's ability to learn.

BACK-TO-BASICS. Movement to strengthen emphasis on basic skills (i.e., the three Rs).

BASAL READERS. Reading texts that teach children to read.

BEHAVIOR MODIFICATION. Goal of many secular humanists to alter child's behavior to fit humanistic ideals of new, atheistic society.

BEHAVIORAL OBJECTIVES. Stated learning goals for individual children.

CATEGORICAL FUNDS. Government funds approved for specific educational projects or programs.

CONSULTANT. Expert in specialized area (educator or otherwise) who provides training, services, and assistance with planning programs and solving problems.

COUNSELOR. Administrative educator responsible to help students with academic planning, discipline, and personal problems.

CULTURALLY DEPRIVED. Students whose home situation has failed to provide minimum cultural enrichment to enable them to fit comfortably into society.

CURRICULUM. Composite of planned lessons, activities, and experiences that make up education. May refer to a single subject area (e.g., English curriculum) or to general curriculum.

CURRICULUM COORDINATOR. Person responsible for planning curriculum, either within a district or a local campus.

CURSIVE WRITING. Form of handwriting used by most adults, in which individual letters are connected within a word.

DIAGNOSTIC TEST. Measures child's strengths and weaknesses in a specific subject or skill area.

DISTRICT SUPERINTENDENT. Chief administrator for all schools in a district.

ED. Cabinet-level federal Department of Education, established in 1980 to replace HEW as seat of federal involvement in education.

ESL. English as Second Language classes for students from homes where English is not primary language.

EXCEPTIONAL CHILD. Any child who learns in a different way to such an extent that he needs special assistance.

FAMILY LIFE EDUCATION. Planned programs of sex education sometimes bear this title.

FUNCTIONAL CURRICULUM. Curriculum of materials that will apply directly to a child's postschool life.

GIFTED CHILD (OR GIFTED AND TALENTED). Child capable of higher than normal performance in academics, creativity, leadership, and/or psychomotor skills.

GOVERNOR'S SCHOOLS. Residential summer programs for gifted students to provide advanced experiences in arts and other academic disciplines.

GROUP THERAPY. Use of role-playing, socio-drama or psycho-drama to break down and change students' behavior patterns and defenses and direct them toward new values.

HANDICAPPED CHILD. Child with physical, mental, or emotional handicap that makes special education necessary. Includes learning disabled, emotionally handicapped, mentally retarded, brain damaged, hyperactive, sensory impaired, other health impaired, minimal brain dysfunction, and many others.

HETEROGENEOUS GROUPING. Practice of mixing students of various abilities together in single classroom or group.

HEW. Federal Department of Health, Education, and Welfare, formerly responsible for federal involvement in education, until establishment of ED in 1980.

HOMOGENEOUS GROUPING. Dividing children into groups according to ability, interest, or achievement level.

IEP. Individualized Education Plan, required by law to be drawn up by educators and parents of handicapped children.

IN-SERVICE TRAINING. Short-term training of educators for specific skills, methods, and/or areas of updated information.

LABELING. Classifying a child as being gifted, a slow learner, a discipline problem, and so on.

LEARNING CENTER. Library of books, audio-visual materials, and other learning aids.

LIBERAL EDUCATION. Broad-based general education in all major areas of study.

MAINSTREAMING. Integrating handicapped children, with their special needs, into classroom of average nonhandicapped learning students.

MANUSCRIPT WRITING. First handwriting a child learns; better known as printing.

MENTOR. Volunteer, trained to teach specific enrichment materials in a classroom.

MINIMUM COMPETENCY TEST. Test of ability to handle basic skills, that all students are required (usually by state law) to pass in order to be promoted or to receive a high school diploma.

NEA. (SEE TEACHER'S ORGANIZATIONS)

NEF. (SEE TEACHER'S ORGANIZATIONS)

NEEDS ASSESSMENT. Survey taken, usually among teachers, parents, community, and/or students to determine existing educational needs.

NORM. Average score a pupil of given age or grade may be expected to make in a standardized test.

NORMALIZATION. Training special children in the most normal schooling situation possible, with the goal of preparing them for post-school experiences in a normal society.

OPEN CLASSROOM. Unstructured classroom environment, where children learn mostly on individual basis or in small groups. Very little used today, it was an experimental method of progressive education.

PHONICS. Method of learning to read by sounding out letters and groups of letters. (*Note:* One highly successful modern program of phonics instruction is the Open Court method.)

PL-94-142. Federal law mandating special education of all handicapped children.

PRINCIPAL. Chief administrator of a school campus. Responsible to manage campus buildings, plan budget, supervise staff and students, and oversee curriculum.

PROGRAMMED TEXT OR PROGRAMMED LEARNING. Planned program of information education using questions and answers. Usually used for individualized instruction.

PROGRESSIVE EDUCATION. Movement headed by John Dewey and William H. Kilpatrick in early twentieth century as protest against traditional, regimented education. Provided increased freedom, encouraged creativity, and minimized rote memory, structured and group learning methods.

PULL-OUT PROGRAM. Program, usually for gifted, in which students are taken out of regular classroom for part of school day, for special activities and/or instruction. Occurs most often on regular basis.

RESOURCE CENTER. *See* LEARNING CENTER.

RESOURCE ROOM. Room where special child goes for part of school day to receive special training to enable him to cope with his handicaps in mainstream classes.

RETENTION. Procedure in which a child is held back so that he must repeat a grade.

ROTE LEARNING. Learning by memorization.

SAT. One of two standard college aptitude tests required of students entering most American colleges or universities (other test is ACT). Measures academic achievement and readiness for college disciplines.

SCHOOL BOARD. Group elected or appointed to be responsible for budgeting, policy making, hiring and firing of personnel, and making schools of a district or county reflect community's wishes.

SCHOOL SITE. Local campus location.

SCHOOL SITE COUNCIL. Special group composed of parents, educators, and sometimes students. Operates on school campus as part of a California program of categorical funding for school improvement. Similar programs exist in several other states as well. Those councils have more action power than advisory councils.

SECULAR HUMANISM. Philosophical position or religion that denies existence of God and moral absolutes and assigns to man the roles and authority traditionally believed to belong to God.

SITUATION ETHICS. Relative moral philosophy that says ethical standards must be altered to fit immediate situation.

SOI. Structure of Intellect thesis proposed by J. P. Guilford "that all children have intelligence in varying degrees and in various abilities" (*see* Resource List under "Gifted").

SPECIAL EDUCATION. Special programs for handicapped students of all kinds.

SPECIALISTS AND ADVISORS. Directors of special education, teachers of special programs (reading, math, and so on), librarians, nurses, and others. They assist teachers and parents.

STANDARDIZED TESTS. Tests given to children all over the country.

TEACHERS' AIDES. Either paid or volunteer helpers who assist educators with wide variety of tasks, either in classroom or elsewhere.

TEACHERS' ORGANIZATIONS.

- AMERICAN FEDERATION OF TEACHERS (AFT). Second largest national teachers' organization in US. Represents almost 25 percent of teachers.
- NATIONAL ASSOCIATION OF PROFESSIONAL EDUCATORS (NAPE). Small organization. Unlike AFT and NEA, it does not support collective bargaining or right to strike.
- NATIONAL EDUCATORS ASSOCIATION (NEA). Largest (nearly 75 percent of all teachers) and most powerful group in the US. Exercises strong lobbying influence on government at all levels.
- NATIONAL EDUCATORS FELLOWSHIP (NEF). Organization of Christian educators (*see* Resource List).

TEAM TEACHING. Classroom situation where two or more teachers share the teaching responsibilities.

UNDERACHIEVER. A child whose academic performance is well below what his aptitude test scores and/or previous performance lead his educators to expect from him.

VALUES CLARIFICATION. Technique that encourages students to examine alternatives to the values they have been taught at home and to establish, often through consensus of peer group opinion, their own values.

VIP. Voluntarily Involved Parent. Anyone, parent or otherwise, who works with schools in a voluntary capacity.

VOCATIONAL EDUCATION. Narrowly focused plan of education, designed to prepare a student for a specific trade or profession.

VOCATIONAL TESTS. Tests that measure either a child's aptitudes or his areas of interest, in order to help him make vocational choices.

VOUCHER PLAN. Proposal to allow parents to choose type of education they desire for their children, to be financed from government funds.

APPENDIX 1

Parish Support for Public Schools*

What can a local pastor do for the children of his congregation who attend public schools? I would like to suggest six possible areas for ministry.

1. Be thankful for the *good* in public education and let those public educators who treat their work as more than just a job know that you appreciate what they are doing. Cultivate good relationships with administrators and teachers, and let them know that as a community leader you support the good they can do. Pray for them—and let them know that you do.

2. Be informed about the problems of public education. While this will happen naturally because of your new relationships, you can also learn about them in other ways. Read about public education; journals such as the *Kappan* or *Educational Leadership* are helpful. Ask parents and students to describe the problems as they see them. Attend PTA meetings when possible. Think the problems through and try to formulate some opinion about them.

3. Establish a relationship with the school-age children in your parish. Invite them for lunch; teach them in a Bible class; do all you can to get to know them and to let them get to know you. Be a model for them who thinks, feels, prays, and lets his Christianity affect everything—even his views on public education.

4. Develop a ministry to families. Seek to strengthen the home and to help open channels of communication between parents and children and the Lord. Show families how they can create an atmosphere of mutual appreciation, concern, growth, and awareness of problems. When you minister to this basic building block of society, you make use of the most natural and influential method God has provided to protect his people against the incursion of evil.

5. Develop educational supplements or alternatives for families and especially for children—and take the ministry of your church's Sunday school program seriously. The sooner we eliminate the Mickey Mouse in church education, the sooner we will experience God's blessings. Work with your teachers to help them become better at their jobs. Make excellence your standard and strive to reach realistic goals in your church.

You might prepare a reading list for parents on the subject of general education, and encourage them to become more informed about its problems and possibilities. Explore the possibility of starting a noon hour Bible study in a home near a local school. Start a class in catechesis. Find other ways to have a *direct* hand in the education of the children in your parish.

6. Finally, pray for your children, and pray for those who, through the public school, exert the second strongest influence upon their lives—an influence that is often stronger than that of the church.

As pastors, we cannot afford to neglect this area of concern. In today's atmosphere of increasing unrest, let us demonstrate that the gospel of Jesus Christ brings stability, purpose, and hope, not only to education, but to all of human life.—T. M. MOORE, minister of education, Coral Ridge Presbyterian Church, Fort Lauderdale, Florida.

APPENDIX 2

A. *Know the three kinds of Parent/Teacher Conferences.*

1. Regularly scheduled conferences. They are an integral part of many schools' program, held early in the school year to acquaint parents with classroom and teacher. If your school does not have this system, make an appointment to get acquainted and talk about your goals and special concerns for your child.

2. Special conferences arising out of problem situations. They are initiated by either teacher or parent. If you see a problem, do not wait. Call the teacher immediately, while the problem is relatively simple to solve. If you cannot arrive at a solution through such a conference, talk with someone else—counselor, principal, or other person close to the situation.

3. Annual Education Check-up at year's end to review a child's records and progress and to consider recommendations for the future of his education. This plan is recommended by NCCE.

B. *Do these things before a conference.*

1. Keep a file of school-related materials for each child. Always review the materials before a conference.

2. Decide in advance what questions you want to ask. Jot them down and take the list with you.

3. Watch your child to note any signs of difficulty (see chapter 7 for more on this subject).

4. Obtain an Annual Education Check-up form from NCCE and study it.

5. Do not drop in for a conference without an appointment.

6. Take advantage of all open houses and other scheduled school functions.

C. *Do these things during the conference.*

1. Approach teacher with warmth, positive attitudes, and honesty. Commend her for things that please you. Let her know you appreciate the role that she is playing in your child's education. Do not be intimidated and fearful to confront her with your legitimate complaints or questions about things you do not understand.

2. Listen to the teacher's side of every issue. Treat her as a respected professional who knows what she is doing. If that is not true, give her the opportunity to prove it.

3. Ask all the questions you need to ask in order to get answers. Find out why your school follows certain procedural patterns. Be persistent until you finally understand. Ask specific questions in order to elicit specific answers.

4. Feel free to express your feelings, concerns, and reactions.

5. Answer the teacher's questions fully and honestly. Remember that you alone know things about your child that just might help to unlock the mysteries and enable the teacher to work out your child's problems.

6. If you feel that the teacher is attacking you or your child unfairly, remain calm under the attack. Make sure she gets all the information she needs to make fair judgments and find workable solutions. In the end, remember that the evaluation of one teacher is not necessarily a final word of authority on your child's needs.

7. Do not let a teacher's educational jargon "snow" you. Insist on a homemaker's English translation of the professional cant that seems so comfortable to her.

8. Be willing to work together with the teacher to find ways that you can both help your child.

9. Offer your assistance, not only with the specific problem of your child but with other kinds of classroom needs as well. Show an interest in the total welfare of the class.

D. *Do these things after the conference.*

1. Carry out recommendations suggested or agreed upon at the conference.

2. Make good on your promises to assist where needed.

3. Report back on evidences of progress or lack of it.

4. Keep in touch.

5. Respect the teacher's confidence in you. Do not turn tidbits of your conversation into gossipy rumors. Be as courteous in her absence as you were in person.

6. Write letters of appreciation to the teacher, sending copies to principal, school board, and district superintendent.

APPENDIX 3

The Television Generation

Stephen T. Hoke*

A quarter of a century ago who would have dreamed that by 1975 more than 60 percent of American families would own two or more television sets or fathomed that young children would average between 15 and 25 hours of television viewing per week? We find television so deeply ingrained in our lives that it is now accepted as an inevitable and ordinary part of daily life. No one imagined the common use of television by parents as a child pacifier, the changes television would bring upon child-rearing methods, the increasing domination of family schedules by children's viewing requirements—in short, the power of the "plug-in drug" to dominate family life.

It is this "early window" that parents are eager to understand, to learn more about, to become aware of its power—both positive and negative. My perspective is that of a new parent, a fellow-television viewer and an educator involved in helping others learn and develop in all areas of life, mental as well as spiritual.

I personally feel that the temptation to single out television as the most pernicious influence of our time is almost irresistable yet irresponsible. To judge television as all bad, with nothing redeeming coming over its airwaves, is to miss the central point of its profound influence by attempting to avoid or forget its presence. The extreme negative position does not offer the most meaningful solution to our dilemma: what do we do with such a pervasive, powerful influencer?

The other extreme is to credit television with nothing but positive and wonderful benefits. This is called the permissive approach, where "the kid can watch anything, it won't hurt him." The child is allowed to sit by the hour watching the video figures mug, murder and mime their way across the stage to the resounding canned laughter of the studio audience.

Analysis

Accurate analysis of the continuous flow of conflicting research data on the effects of television viewing is a difficult task. By the

*Stephen Hoke is assistant professor of religion at Seattle Pacific University. He holds the M.A. in missions from Wheaton Graduate School, the Master of Divinity from Trinity Evangelical Divinity School, and the Ph.D. in education from Michigan State University. This article appeared in *Voices,* Winter 1979, pp. 12-15, and is used by permission.

time a child has finished high school he or she has spent 10,800 hours in the classrooms and over 15,000 hours watching television. The Broadcasting Yearbook of 1971 estimated that the average American television set is turned on 6 hours and 18 minutes per day; another study described the average American spending 20 hours a week watching the tube, while the average set is on 8 or 9 hours every day.

Preschool children are the single largest television audience in America, spending a greater number of total hours and a greater proportion of their waking day watching television than any other age group. On Saturday morning children may be bombarded by 5½ hours of mesmerizing video on all three major networks. However, less than 10 percent of a child's viewing occurs on Saturday mornings. The other 90 percent of children's viewing includes programming planned for adult audiences during daytime television throughout the week.

It is only in the last few years that most of us, parents, educators and broadcasters alike, have realized just how sizable a role television plays in the lives of our children. The realization has been a sobering one.

EDUCATIONAL IMPLICATIONS

It is vitally important that parents and other adults working with television-viewing children see the big picture of where television fits into the scheme of family life and growth together. The Christian's view of the family is based on principles and considerations not necessarily held by mankind in general. Christians believe that the family is a God-given institution with a divine commission and responsibility for the nurturing of the child's mental, spiritual and physical development. For a Christian, no human relationship is more significant than one's family.

Two crucial contributions of the family are directly related to the moral and spiritual development of children. First, the family provides environments which nurture growth and development. These environments contribute toward a sense of security, identity and personal worth. They foster dialogue and interaction with the child, and this contributes toward a rational understanding of self and others. The home must also provide an environment of equity and justice—where the child can experience fairness. This experience contributes toward the child's developing a sense of righteousness as justice with love.

Second, the family provides models which prefigure the child's awareness of God. A mother and father united in loving marriage provide for nurturance in their very relationship with one another and with the child. From the parents the child learns about love, communication and how to relate to others. He or she sees the principles of morality, right and wrong, and justice lived out and exemplified before him or her. The child begins to learn right behavior from the kinds of behaviors seen in her or his parents. It is in the context of a loving home that a child's emerging behavior can be influenced and corrected.

The unfortunate fact is that most Christian parents have no idea how much time their children spend watching television. According to the St. Clement Film Society, "Churchmen join with the rest in spending more time looking at television than they do at any other activity aside from sleeping and working." Television has and will continue to have a profound effect on family life until concerned parents take the initiative in planning and structuring family life to build relationships between family members and sever the relationship long-established between the electric friend with the glass face.

A team of Christian educators at Michigan State University has taken the findings of Psychologists Lawrence Kohlberg and Jean Piaget and suggested several important educational implications for parents. First, realize that the modes or roles of moral influence used by parents must change over time. As the child develops in mental ability, for example, he or she will be able to comprehend and respond to increasingly sophisticated messages and instructions from parents and others. At first children will need the nurture of rewards and punishments handled in a just manner. Then they will begin to respond to examples. Develop with children an orderly use of rules; not as a basis for punishment, but to enhance confidence and communication by clarifying the expectations and demands of the just and secure environment of home.

Second, develop a relationship with your children in which open dialogue and rich experiences are continually shared. Thus will you be ready to provide the needed comfort and encouragement when your child reaches a time of disequilibrium.

Rather than providing the mode of moral influence appropriate with the child's level of moral development, television often provides examples of behavior and language that contradict the child's understanding of right and wrong. Where does the young child see behavior that is reprimanded or corrected in relation to some source of authority or standard of morality? Right behavior is rarely rewarded; wrong behavior is punished only infrequently. The models offered are ficticious wizards of electronic morality often not dealing with real-life issues for children and adolescents. Rules are too often scoffed at and belittled by young and old alike, from "Kotter's" kids to "Family's" teens. Reasons for right or wrong behavior and explanations of the principles affecting human life are left to the last several minutes of television programs.

NEGATIVE FEATURES

I have already mentioned generally that television's contribution to family life has been a disruptive one. It may be helpful to document briefly several specific negative effects of television on a child's development: social interaction and direct experience.

The "Garbage In—Garbage Out" principle is in effect when considering the influence of television's input on children. Although I am not equating children with computers, our mental storage capabilities will reflect the quality and quantity of the input we receive. Any external influence of fifteen to twenty-five hours a week will, by sheer quantity of time, have an impact upon one's mind and life!

Regardless of content, excessive viewing inhibits development. The developing child needs opportunities to discover and build basic family relationships, thereby coming to understand herself or himself flexibly and clearly, in order to function as a social creature. The television experience does not further verbal development because it does not require verbal participation, merely passive intake. The hours that the young child or adolescent spends in a one-way relationship with television people, definitely affects that child's relationships with real-life people, especially other family members. Studies show the importance of eye-to-eye contact in real-life relationships, although in certain children's programs people purport to speak directly to the child. How might such a distortion of real-life relationships affect a child's development of trust, of openness, of an ability to relate well to other real people? Bruno Bettelheim writes: "Children who have been taught, or conditioned, to listen passively most of the day to the warm verbal communications coming from the TV screen, to the deep emotional appeal of the so-called TV personality, are often unable to respond to real persons because they arouse so much less feeling than the skilled actor. Worse, they lose the ability to learn from reality because life experiences are much more complicated than the ones they see on the screen. . . ."

But more obviously damaging to family relationships is the elimination of opportunities to talk, and perhaps more important, to argue, between parents and children and brothers and sisters. Families frequently use television to avoid confronting their problems, problems that will not go away if they are ignored but will only fester and become less easily resolved as time passes. The child's early and increased television experiences decrease the opportunities for simple conversation between parents and children and will serve to dehumanize, mechanize, and make less real the relationships she or he encounters in life. Television has played an important role in the disintegration of the American famly in its effect on family relationships, its facilitation of parental withdrawal from an active role in the socialization of their children, and in its replacement of family rituals and special events.

Secondly, television viewing undercuts learning. Until the television era a young child entered the world of fantasy primarily by way of stories told or read from a book. But rarely did such literary experiences take up a significant proportion of a child's waking time; an hour or so a day was more time than most children spent caught up in the imagination of others.

Now, by means of television, very young children enter and spend sizable portions of their waking time in a secondary world of make-believe people and intangible things, unaccompanied, in too many cases, by an adult guide or comforter. The nature of the two experiences is different, and that difference significantly affects the impact of the material taken in.

In reading, the mind transforms abstract symbols into sounds and the sounds into words; it "hears" the words, as it were, and invests them with meanings learned in the spoken language. We create our own images when reading based on our life experiences and reflecting on our own needs, while we must accept what we receive when watching television images at the pace of the imagination of the show's creators.

In a recent conference for young authors at Seattle Pacific University, the content of the books and articles written by children in elementary school gave overwhelming indication of the influence of television on the minds of these young writers. The majority of the main characters and plots of the stories were taken from or adaptations of television programs. Their ability to creatively visualize had been significantly retarded by television watching. Unfortunately, there is no doubt that children read fewer books when television is available to them.

Thirdly, television confuses reality and fantasy. As a young child's "early window," television is a remarkable invention that is clearly changing everybody's world. Dorothy Cohen, professor of child development at Bank Street College of Education, highlights the fact that "children have difficulty distinguishing between program content and commercials; distinguishing relevant for irrelevant detail; and figuring the central informational themes of a program." Cohen points the finger of blame on television for our continued prejudicial stereotypes of women, the prevalence of police and detectives, misunderstandings of minority racial groups, and the distortion of the lifestyle of minority groups.

In one analysis of 16 popular programs and 216 commercials, men outnumbered women by three to one; females were more often shown in instances of negative behavior than males; females were twice as likely to show incompetence; and the male was most frequently the sole source of economic support. Unfortunately, attempts to right the imbalance of the sexes on television are often clumsy, (e.g. "Bionic Woman," "Police Woman," "Charlie's Angels"). Fully half of all leading television characters fall in the category of the white, American male, usually young, middle-class, unmarried and likely to be involved in violence, especially as an aggressor rather than as a victim. Eight percent of all characters were found to be white Americans. Of the 20 percent remaining, Europeans were the ethnic group appearing most frequently. Foreigners and minorities in the 1969 study were more likely than Anglo-Americans to be law breakers.

The subject of television violence and its potential affect on children has long been a source of controversy. The intense interest in the influence of violence stems understandably from the exponential increase in juvenile crimes between 1952 and 1972—over 1,600 percent. This is the very period in which television appeared in the home of almost every American.

Is it merely a coincidence that the entry of television into the American home brought in its wake one of the worst epidemics of juvenile violence in the nation's history? There are indeed reasons to believe that television is deeply implicated in the new upsurge of juvenile aggression.

The problem is not that children and adolescents learn how to commit violence from watching violence on television, but that television conditions them to deal with real people as if they were on a television screen. They are able to "turn them off," quite simply, with a knife, gun or chain, with as little remorse as if they were turning off a television set.

The overwhelming message violent programs communicate according to Victor Cline, professor of psychology at the University of Utah, is that violence pays. Violence is the way to get what you want. Networks have been criticized for claiming their violent programs demonstrate crime doesn't pay, but only alluding to this fact during the last five minutes of the program. For forty-five minutes the kid watches how the criminal profits.

Positive Features

I am uneasy with an evaluation of television which looks only at its negative influence. There are also several powerful positive effects of the electric education television provides. First, it provides a greatly enlarged window on the world than was previously available for young children. Through world news coverage, on-the-spot reporting of unusual events and natural phenomena, and highly refined photographic techniques, television has opened up vast vistas of knowledge and scientific technology. A video-literate child of the seventies has been privileged to see village life in Africa, cultural exchange programs with Japan and China, entertainment from Europe, animal life in the jungles of Africa, earthquakes and volcanic eruptions from the South Pacific and childbirth in the United States. He or she has seen man walk on the moon, poverty in Biafra and Bangladesh, political violence in Italy, ice skating in Moscow, sabotage in Munich and thriller commando raids at Antebbe.

Second, television provides an enormous amount of high quality entertainment for children and adults alike. While sitting on the family floor young children can experience the thrill of sitting front row at Carnegie Hall to hear Beverly Sills, the Boston Pops, Leonard Bernstein conducting noted orchestras, the Metropolitan opera, watch the saga of "Roots," enjoy the best of European circuses, learn from the finest performances of world-class athletes in gymnastics, track and field and winter sports. Television can enrich the vicarious experience of youngsters in most areas of the fine and performing arts, including drama, musicals, orchestra, opera and special concerts.

Third, for schoolagers, television wisely and selectively used as a part of family or group activity with follow-up discussion, can be a highly useful and entertaining educational tool. Certain programs are particularly designed to engender speculative thought in children and the investigation of their feelings and can make a unique and valuable contribution to their emotional and intellectual development.

Many shows stretch the imagination and vision of children confined to four-walled classrooms to consider the globe as their laboratory and the nation as their resource center. Parents watching with their children can turn to public and commercial television to see increasingly useful and valuable programs on science, art, environmental studies, music, literature and history. The limitations in finances and facilities of one's neighborhood school can be supplemented by the multi-million dollar labs of universities and NASA.

In light of the enormous influence of television, what can a Christian parent do? The following suggestions may offer concrete advice for parents on the brink of decision whether to throw away the television set or purchase a new color receiver with quadraphonic sound.

1. Take the initiative. Many of the difficulties parents encounter in controlling their children's television watching are compounded by a lack of certainty about what role they wish television to play in their family life and a basic ambivalence about television. The account of countless parents who share their anger, worry and frustration in monitoring television gives evidence that real conviction is a basic requirement for successful use. When the parents' game-plan for family life is presented and developed with the children, it must be shared with conviction. James Dobson and other Christian writers on the family share the importance of parental action and initiative done in a spirit of love and kindness.

2. Study and learn about television; don't just react. The first step is to find out what is going on: How much television are your children watching? What are they watching? When are they watching? A good way to assess present viewing patterns in your home is to keep a notebook by the set for a week and have them write down the hours the set is on and the programs they see. At the end of the week, total up the hours and look over the programs. If you are

unhappy with the results, it is vitally important to share your concern with the family. It may open up a discussion of disturbing things they have seen.

More importantly, I am suggesting that Christian parents begin to inform and educate themselves about this most powerful of contemporary media. Articles, studies and books abound in your local library. Don't be content to swallow all the negative charges of articles in Christian magazines, even ones like this article. Review the statistics, follow the trends, reflect on your experience and discuss it with your family and friends.

3. Provide a balanced diet of nurturant environments and experiences. Television is only one of a myriad number of discovery experiences for children which will enhance their learning and understanding of themselves and the world around them. By default we have let them assume it is the most important learning experience; but it is not. Work, play, travel, field trips, radio listening, reading, writing and daydreaming are but a few of the types of experiences that nurture a child's early development in the physical, social, mental and spiritual dimensions.

55–Schools: How Parents Can Show They Care

Work together to plan family activities. Prayer together will help focus all minds on the centrality of Christ in the family life. Talk through the options and activities available in your area for discovery, investigation, trips and play. Observe your children's different abilities and interests and plan outings and experiences which will capture the interest of each child's unique skills and gifts. Involve your children in decision-making about their after-school and leisure-time activities, including television watching. Working as a family unit to creatively design learning and recreational times will help keep television in perspective. Family nights at home with games, concerts, readings and special surprises will quickly supplant the omnipresent glow of the tube.

One mother described how one day, while being assaulted by the hysterical laughter of a captive quiz-show audience, she finally shouted, "I demand equal time." She then devised an ingenious plan based on her children's competitiveness and red-blooded response to a challenge. The plan required her children to put in equal time working, playing, reading or engaging in an alternative activity for the same amount of time their favorite show lasted. Beginning with only 15 minutes of Beethoven traded for equal time with the "Brady

Bunch," she watched her children and family regain the satisfaction of accomplishing and reaping the rewards of work. She observed fewer arguments over which child watched what show, until finally silence resounded from wall to wall. Within several weeks the television had virtually been stilled. Both children had developed a love for reading.

4. Teach your children *how* to watch television and give them reasons *why*. Young children have limited understanding of what is good for them and what is bad. They need to be helped in deciding what to eat, how much to sleep, what to wear, as well as what to watch and where to play. At first you will want to restrict the number of hours they watch, but from the beginning you can begin to share your thinking and reasons for limited viewing and the advantages of engaging in other activities.

The best way for parents to teach their children balanced viewing is to set the example. Providing adequate models is crucial for children of any age. Children still model most of their behavior after their parents, so you have to be prepared to turn the set off and pick up a book yourself. Model the desired behavior. In contrast to the media which melts half-truths into fact and purposely mislead in advertising, we must be honest with children, willing to give direct, honest answers to our children's questions. This is all a part of the behavior we model.

Comment on things you see with your children. Just as parents often comment on bedtime stories read to children, so even the smallest remark can make a difference in the effect a television episode has on your children. Use your family television viewing as a basis for conversation. When serious discussions become difficult in the growing-up years, personal feelings and experiences can sometimes be unlocked if parents will use similar situations seen on television to initiate dialogue with their children.

5. Make your feelings and convictions about television known in your community. Parents concerned with program content and commercialism can make an impact on network producers. A group of agitated parents in Boston got together to explore ways to make television live up to its potential. This small group of suburban mothers has grown into Action for Children's Television (ACT) with representatives in over fifty cities and has already been successful in reducing the amount of advertising to children by 40 percent. In addition, ACT has succeeded in eliminating "host selling," where the

children's favorite performer sells the sponsor's product. Two more grass-roots parent organizations in New York and Iowa have worked with local stations to develop more instructional programs.

Whether a child watches five hours of television a week or twenty-five, television viewing is an important part of his or her life. The quality of television viewing will only be as good as the use to which programs are put in the home. For parents who pay little or no attention to their children's viewing, television is no more than an electric babysitter, an informative and entertaining technological tool whose value will vary from child to child in unpredictable—and sometimes undesirable fashion.

But for parents who grasp firmly their share of the responsibility and who actively involve themselves in their children's viewing experience, television can be—and will be—a significant and constructive contributor to the growth and development of this "television generation" of young people.

APPENDIX 4

KEY COMMUNICATORS

*Don Bagin**

The concept of "key communicators" is probably not an innovative one for some school officials. Many educators have applied the ideas behind the key communicator approach in their schools. Few, however, have formalized it in the manner suggested here.

Why do we need key communicators? Too often in almost every community rumors get out of hand. In many cases, such rumors, although unfounded, have resulted in the dismissal of school administrators. Usually the rumors could have been quickly ended in their early stages. However, in too many cases, the rumors grew and grew, causing what was a spark to become a raging fire. One example that occurred a few years ago in a suburban district located near a ghetto demonstrates the need for key communicators.

What can happen without key communicators? Ten people appeared at the superintendent's office. They brought a petition signed by 1200 people—a petition protesting and opposing the plans to bus children from that district (which was upper middle class) to a nearby city school district. They brought reporters and a TV cameraman with them. The superintendent was surprised. He had no inkling that there was such community concern. In fact, he did not know that the petition was being circulated. The media, of course, had a page one story, even though the superintendent candidly denied that any such plans had been discussed. (And this was the truth.) One person had misconstrued a statement made by another school official and the rumor spread. Not one of the 1200 people signing the petition talked with anyone from the school to get the facts. All, it appears, assumed the petition statement was correct.

Are there examples of the key communicators' idea working? Many school administrators are glad to share their successes as a result of implementing the key communicator concept. Here are examples from three communities.

Example One

A black ninth grade student and a white ninth grade student fought in the junior high school building during the school day. The

---

*Don Bagin is coordinator, Graduate School Communications Program, Glassboro State College, Glassboro, New Jersey.

black student was suspended; the white student was not. Given just those facts, the community justifiably could have been upset; in fact, a riot could have ensued. The additional facts were that the black student had engaged in two previous fights and he and his parents had been told that one more fight would necessitate suspension. The fight was the first for the other student.

The key communicators helped the principal avoid any problems as they were told the facts and they shared them with the people they talked with.

Example Two

A senior on the night of the senior prom was seen trying to climb the left field wall of the high school baseball field—at midnight—in his tux. This was considered unusual for that community, and the rumors would probably have had the entire class on an LSD trip. Only the one student was on such a trip, however.

The key communicators communicated that fact to the rest of the community, thereby avoiding what could have been a major problem for school administrators and for students in homes throughout the district.

Example Three

The day before a tax levy election in a county school district, the county newspaper ran an accurate article that was given page-one position. The article was favorable in showing the district's needs in a fair manner but the headline was totally misleading.

School officials didn't have time to prepare a formal response of any kind. Furthermore, they did not want to alienate the newspaper by complaining about the poor headline.

Key communicators came into play here by spreading the word that the story and its salient points were excellent, but that the headline was misleading. Facts were provided to the key communicators, showing how the headline was inconsistent with the facts in the story. Also provided was some brief background on the time pressures of preparing a headline that must fit a certain space.

How did the information get to the key communicators? An administrator is charged with the responsibility of communicating with the key communicators on a district-wide basis. This administrator began a telephone chain that had been established for this purpose. When time permits, a written statement can be distributed.

Are key communicators for district-wide use or should they be set up on a school basis? Both ways work. Some school districts do it strictly through the superintendent's office. In this case, principals are usually asked to help identify people who can serve as key communicators. In other districts, each principal is responsible for setting up a key communicator network. It is of course possible for the superintendent to identify his key communicator group from members of the principals' groups.

What kind of a person should a key communicator be? Any person who talks to a large number of people should be considered for key communicator designation. If the person is believed and trusted by large numbers of people, that person should definitely be asked to serve. The person need not have the usual formal power-structure kind of status that we too often seek for school help. The person might be a barber, a beautician or a bartender. The person might own a hoagie shop or be a school crossing guard. Or a postmaster or a gas station operator. In any event, he or she should be talking to a large number of people in the community.

It's important to identify key communicators who will talk to all the different segments of the community. In some communities, it might be difficult to identify key communicators, especially in new developments that have not yet evolved their power structure. In this case, people can be asked to serve as key communicators to tell the school story and to report rumors. Usually the people do then become key communicators in that development.

Should there be key communicators in the schools? Definitely. A group of student and staff key communicators can add much to the overall communications effort. As shown in study after study, students and employees are prime sources of information about the schools. Therefore, it's imperative that all who are in the school know the facts before they return home to share their information with other people. Again, these people should be chosen in a way that assures getting the word to all segments of the student body and the staff.

In addition to using key communicators to spread the facts, how can they help? Key communicators can identify the sparks before they become fires. Members of the group must be encouraged to call school officials with questions they have. Or with questions or concerns they have heard from neighbors, friends or customers.

For example, Harry the Barber might be told by a customer that the proposed new high school is going to cost $10 million. Harry calls the superintendent and finds that the cost will be $7 million. How many people will Harry help know the facts. How many people will the people Harry told tell? It's got to help.

Key communicators must have the right to call the administrator with whom they are working with a rumor or question. This kind of freedom, although now technically available to all people, must be clearly communicated.

Some school districts call a meeting of key communicators before making a major decision. Some use the group to get ideas and reactions before presenting a budget or a bond issue to the remainder of the community. Some get the group's thinking on issues like busing and the extended school year before going to the rest of the community.

In fact, one of the ongoing bonuses is the ability to get the pulse of the community rather quickly by asking the key communicators their opinions regarding almost any educational issue.

Doesn't setting up the key communicators take time? Of course it does. In fact, most administrators are reluctant to take the time because they understandably see it subtracting from the already limited time they have for other responsibilities. At the end of a year, however, almost all administrators agree that the existence of the key communicators saves more time than it takes. Major crises have been eliminated and people now get the facts before criticizing the schools, administrators report.

How does a school start the key communicators idea? If the superintendent decides to begin such a program, ordinarily a list of people would be compiled by various employees independently. A demographic look at the community would be taken to make sure that various groups would have someone on the list. The lists would be considered and people chosen. Usually the same names appear on many lists.

The superintendent then sends a letter to each person advising that the person has been selected and explaining the nature of the organization—to help improve schools through better communication. The superintendent then calls each member and invites him or her to a small-group meeting with about seven other key communicators. The personal phone call usually brings from 85% to 95% attendance. The secretary's phone call usually results in about 60% to

75% attendance and the letter only will usually attract about half the people invited.

At the luncheon or other get-together, the tone is informal. No formal agenda is prepared and the time pressures of all involved are respected. This means that the meeting is held to 60 or 75 minutes at the most. People get to know the superintendent and the superintendent gets to know them. It's really a confidence-building session that allows people to see that the chief executive is a person who cares about kids, understands that problems exist, and seems to be doing the best possible job to solve them. Also, that the superintendent is receptive to ideas and encourages questions and suggestions. People are asked to call when they hear a rumor and are told that they will be apprised of information about the schools when a problem or challenge or need exists.

Perhaps once a year, the entire group of key communicators will be called together for a meeting (budget or bond issue or test score results consideration). This enables them to see that other people in the community care enough about the school to give time to help communicate.

(The ideas given above can be used by a principal to set up the key communicators in a school.)

How many people should be on such a team? It varies from district to district. Some small districts might use only 15 or 20 people. Others may use 20 people for each school. The number is not the key; if, for instance, a person feels slighted and wants to be a member, add one more. Every person can help in some way. It is unusual that a person who gets involved in the schools in this way does not aid the school's program either directly or indirectly.

In an age of a lack of public confidence in public officials, any attempt to communicate honestly and openly will be applauded. This program can do just that. More importantly, it can help improve education.

APPENDIX 5

A. *How to recruit members*

1. *Talk about your concern* at coffees, through newspaper articles, letters to editors, in form letters, at social occasions, wherever you mix with people. Recruit widely. If you send form letters, follow them up with telephone calls or visits. One-on-one communication is still the most effective recruiting method.

2. *Follow up all leads.* When you talk with people, ask them for further leads. Keep eyes open for people doing things that indicate an interest in your project. Ask educators and your children for leads.

3. *Ask prospective recruits for a commitment,* not to you, but to a task. If they are Christians, present it as a commitment to the Lord and His work.

4. *Make clear the terms of your requested involvement.* Never say to a person: "There's really nothing to this job." That is false bait. If it should be true, who wants to waste his time on an organization that does nothing?

B. *Recognize needs of parent groups*

1. *Purpose and goals.* Make sure you are tackling real problems, not just picky pet peeves. Be an action group, not a gripers' club.

2. *Structure.*

   a) Organization with enough leadership in different areas of concern to get the job done, but no more leaders than are needed.

   b) Meetings need structure too. Set and observe realistic, comfortable time limits. Start and stop on time. Operate meetings with an agenda. Do not be so rigid that members feel it is the leaders' group, not theirs.

3. *Enthusiastic leadership.* A must in order to keep members encouraged, inspired, but not driven.

4. *Lively meetings.* Any meeting of busy parents must compete with the fast-paced drama of the media and of hectic daily schedules. Make your group significant and lively—well worth the priority members will have to give it.

5. *Teamwork spirit.* Take time to warm up to each other, to practice becoming a unified body, to get acquainted and to feel comfortable with each other.

6. *Shared responsibilities.* When a subject is too big for the whole group to handle at once, break up into task forces. Find out what each member prefers to do (e.g., stuff envelopes or telephone absentees), and try to assign tasks accordingly. Do not overwork a few faithful souls, but draw out all members. There is strength in diversity of talents and interests.

7. *Shared ideas.* Use brainstorming techniques when searching for solutions to problems. Increases creativity immensely.

8. *Job training.* Particularly in a continuing group, train new members in group history, organizational structure, purposes, and goals. Take time to bring in consultants to train members in background information on specific problems or in techniques for solving specific problems.

9. *Appreciation.* Letters of thanks, plaques awarded at the end of specific projects, appreciation dinners, even small words dropped at meetings, on the telephone, or in social contacts pay off in member eagerness to participate.

C. *Some important don'ts:*

1. *Don't cajole or trick hesitant recruits* into joining or doing a job. Be honest and respect the individual's right to say no. Never tell a person, "God has revealed to me that you are to do this job." Let God reveal His will directly to the person He has chosen.

2. *Don't fear controversial issues.* Talk them out. Encourage honest examination of a subject. Never ridicule or belittle a person when he expresses a view not held by the majority.

3. *Don't fear failure.* Failure is often the only route by which you can reach success. It can certainly bring learning if we accept it as the material upon which to build solutions.

4. *Don't insist on pushing through your pet project* without a solid base of support from your group.

5. *Don't allow a bossy leader to ruin a group* or a specific project by insisting on being the show.

6. *Don't be afraid to evaluate your work* and determine both problems and successes.

APPENDIX 6

How to Write a Letter for Action

1. *Address the right person/persons.* You may want to send copies to other persons concerned with your issue, but make sure your letter is principally addressed to the person who can help you the most. Remember to work up through the chain of command.

2. *Be original.* Duplicated or carbon letters give the impression that you were emotionally drawn onto a bandwagon without any understanding of the real issues.

3. *Use a businesslike tone.* Avoid emotional outbursts, accusations, and ultimatums. Be polite and show restraint and understanding of the other person's positions.

4. *Make your letter look professional.* Type it if you can, or have a friend type it for you. If that is impossible, write legibly and neatly on clean, plain paper. Fancy or perfumed stationery rarely makes a good impression and may even give the recipient a headache if he is allergic to your perfume.

5. *Focus your efforts.* Do not send a thirty-page document, listing 150 personal grievances against the school district. Deal with one vital issue at a time.

6. *Be positive.* Be sure to commend where possible, but only as it applies—not for apple-polishing. Give definite reasons why you believe what you believe.

7. *Keep it brief.* Time is limited for the professional educator, board member, or politician. He is more likely to read and react favorably to what you say if he can read it quickly.

8. *State your objective clearly.* Give evidence that you have studied the subject. Then indicate what specific action you want taken.

9. *Always sign your name and address.* If writing as a representative of a group, say so and name the group, but be sure to indicate your own name as well.

10. *Say Thank you.* When you receive a reply, and especially when the desired action follows, be as eager and prompt to say, "Thank you," as you were to yell, "Help!"

APPENDIX 7

1. Improve student and teacher attendance, thereby increasing state revenue for students and decreasing the cost of substitute teachers.

2. Support state adjustment legislation that increases allotments to students with special needs and softens the blow to budgets of schools with declining enrollment.

3. Compare the cost of contracted services (food, transportation, maintenance) with services provided by the school system.

4. Set priorities for spending. Explore ways to shift more school dollars to instructional and classroom areas.

5. Evaluate local taxes to find out if they are too high. How do they compare with taxes in districts of the same size?

6. Compare school program costs with other similar districts to see if they are in line.

7. Use attrition to gradually reduce staff without violating union contracts.

8. Seek new sources of local revenue besides property tax (wage tax, income tax, occupation tax, mercantile tax, sales tax, per capita tax). Compare the business profit rate with corporate tax rate in your area to determine if business is paying its fair share.

9. Check the efficiency of each department. Are you getting your money's worth in the areas of transportation, maintenance?

10. Compare expenditures for the past several years to determine which are increasing faster than the rate of inflation.

11. Make a tally sheet showing how much money can be saved by closing a school. Don't forget that some costs may continue or actually rise.

12. Stop penalizing departments for being frugal and underspending their budgets. Do not reduce line items for the next year simply because a surplus existed this year.

13. Spend your time wisely looking for budget cuts that really count, and don't be deflected away from officials' pet projects. Consider all the alternatives before cutting the budget.

*Network, April 1979, p. 3, and September 1979, p. 6, published by the National Committee for Citizens in Education, 410 Wilde Lake Village Green, Columbia, MD 21044. Used by permission.

14. Consider reorganization of attendance areas, grade division, and consolidation of schools, or use cooperative state agencies to provide special services to small districts without losing local identity.

15. Make administrative dollars count. Use administrators to cover classrooms when teachers are absent or experiment with using one principal for two small schools as an alternative to closing one.

16. Investigate conflicts of interest by school officials that may make contracted goods or services cost more than they should.

17. Use competitive bidding for employee health insurance contracts. Some insurers have "sweetheart" deals with the teachers' unions so you may have to weather an unfair labor practice charge, but it does save money without cutting benefits.

18. Form a self-insured pool with nearby districts for unemployment insurance, industrial accidents, liability, fire and vandalism, and so on.

19. Examine usage of substitute teachers. Are they paid for half or whole days when needed for only one or two hours?

APPENDIX 8

"Would a State Voucher System Work?"

Yes: Vouchers Let Parents Choose Best School for Their Children

*John E. Coons**

Yes, a voucher system would work, if designed like the proposal being debated in California. Its three principal objectives are the child's best interest, racial integration, and civil tolerance.

Today these goals often are frustrated by a depersonalized, cumbersome, and elitist system. The wealthy choose schools by changing residence or buying private education; for the rest assignment is compulsory. Would choices by ordinary parents be worse than assignments imposed arbitrarily by residence? Rationality would suggest the opposite. When protected by minimum standards and adequate counseling, the family is plainly the best agent to link the child to the right teacher and school.

The California proposal preserves the traditional public schools, but no longer would their audience be captive. Families would qualify for scholarships redeemable by two kinds of certified schools— public and private scholarship schools. The former would be separate public corporations with increased faculty control. Similar rules would govern public and private scholarship schools, but some special advantages would be retained for the traditional public schools.

Scholarship schools would accept all applicants, using random selection if oversubscribed. A system of due process would prevent discrimination. Transport would be provided, and a personalized information system would help families make choices.

Scholarships would vary by need and cost; larger scholarships would reward children in integrated schools. Tuition would be forbidden except in the form of supplementary state scholarships sold at prices adjusted to family size and income.

Voluntary integration could stretch beyond court orders, producing more stable interracial schools. Those subordinated in the present system would have their views respected, and trust would beget trust. Family choice is a basic investment in social harmony.

*John E. Coons is professor of law at the University of California, Berkeley.

Finally, choice is also enlightened self-interest for the educator, since the health of publicly financed education ultimately depends upon its serving clients as well as managers. Private schools in California have recently increased their share of pupils from 6 to greater than 10 percent.

We must provide access to all schools for all income classes, or education will continue to be both a depressed industry and an agent of segregation.

No: Vouchers Lead to Less Equality, Require Costly Bureaucracy

*Ruth B. Love**

Giving tax money directly to parents who can then spend their voucher at any school sounds reasonable on the surface. Yet when one looks closely at a proposed constitutional amendment here in California, serious problems become apparent.

There are moral questions. Middle and upper-class parents, as "sophisticated consumers," are likely to have more time, inclination, and expertise than poor people in "shopping" for schools for their children.

The educational marketplace or freedom-of-choice concept inherent in the voucher plan poses a substantial threat to the democratic ideal of equal opportunity. This plan would negate our nation's attempt to educate the children of the masses. It would leave only poor children in the public schools, at a time when other nations of the world strive toward universal education.

As adults select schools based on their own value systems there is certain to be an increase in segregation by race, class, religion, and ideology, thus destroying the public schools traditional function in building cohesiveness in our society. Voucher plans would give free reign to racism, classism, and sexism denying children a chance to learn a very basic skill—respect for diversity.

Then, there is the serious constitutional question of providing funds—even indirectly—for religion in schools. The California proposal and most other voucher systems now being considered nationwide make private and parochial schools eligible to participate on the grounds that without them there is an abridgement of freedom of

*Formerly superintendent of public schools, Oakland, California, Ruth B. Love is presently superintendent of public schools, Chicago, Illinois.

choice. But with them there is certainly a possible violation of the first amendment. The statewide voucher system as proposed would surely deny equal access to quality education, thereby violating equal protection under the law.

Another major objection is financial. The astronomical cost of funding the massive new bureaucracy required to set up and monitor a voucher plan would have to be met by new taxes and would ultimately drain funds from public schools and bankrupt the state treasury.

Finally, vouchers would be an administrative nightmare. Enrollment figures would be uncertain and planning difficult.

Undoubtedly, education must improve. But there is no reasonable guarantee that vouchers can accomplish it. Public education can and should offer choices, but equally as important, every school should be challenged to offer first-class comprehensive education.

Reprinted from "Would a State Voucher System Work?" *Instructor*, May 1979. © 1979 by The Instructor Publications, Inc. Used by permission.

APPENDIX 9

(Yogic sequential exercises are imposed on children in Minnesota schools to modify behavior. It is the practice of a pagan ritual. Beware!)

Transcendental Meditation (TM), is called by its adherents, the foundation for a more energetic, successful life. They claim that TM "is dynamic action from deep rest". Adherents say that TM deals positively with EVERY social and physical ill of our age. Adherents state that TM has nothing to do with religion. In the face of the massive media endorsement of TM and by the public at large, it is well to examine TM in some detail.

The TM movement was initially called the Spiritual Regeneration Movement. Regeneration is a prime attribute of the Hindu holy Trinity, in particular the god Vishnu.

The philosophy underlying TM, is called the Science of Creative Intelligence (SCI).

The Maharishi Mahesh Yogi became world famous after indoctrinating the Beatles and Mia Farrow with TM at a "camp" in India. Victor Kulanday, a Hindu Swami, said the "camp" deteriorated into a sexual orgy.[1]

The same Kulanday, states that TM stimulates the psychic centers of the body, which leads to sexual disorders.[2]

SCI, the philosophy underlying TM, is a revival of ancient Indian Brahmanism and Hinduism.[3] This philosophy is point for point identical to Vedantic Hinduism.[4]

The Maharishi Mahesh Yogi is, himself, of the Shankara tradition of Hinduism, which by definition is Vedantic Hinduism.

The Swami Kulanday states that the very TM initiation ceremony is a purely orthodox Hindu religious ceremony. And further, the Swami states that every time a TM pupil invokes the "secret word" (Mantra), he is invoking a spirit to possess him.[5] The Christian Hindu Kulanday would substitute for TM, his Vital Energy System (VES), based upon the same pagan Hindu religion.

212

TM, with its emphasis on meditation, the use of a Mantra and concentration on a single object is a variant of the Hindu practice of Yoga, packaged for consumption in the western world.

Yoga, from the Sanskrit root "Yug", literally means to yoke or unite the human soul with the universal spirit. Yoga is one of SIX systems in understanding the Upanishads, the mystical interpretations of the Veda. The resultant of any one of these systems is the "Dharma", or "Universal Moral Order". Yoga seeks to liberate the individual from the "cycle of re-birth" or reincarnation, which to the Hindu constitutes salvation.

The Maharishi, himself, states that TM presents ancient Vedic wisdom in acceptable western terms.[6]

The Veda, Aryan or classical Sanskrit writings, is the heart of Hinduism.

The Mantra of TM is called the "Bija Mantra", or literally "Seed Mantra," which is common to most eclectic Yoga systems.

Mantras, or hymns of the Vedas, are the purposeful recitation of magical spells or incantations and, according to the Maharishi, are used to produce an effect in another world, ". . . to draw the attention of these higher beings or gods living there."[7]

The use of the Mantras is based upon "Mantra Yoga" or "Yoga of Spells", a medieval variant of "Raja" or "Royal" Yoga, that teaches the continual repetition of magical phrases as a means of disassociating consciousness.

Mantras, or hymns of the Vedas, are taken from the second part of the Veda, called Atharva-Veda, which is a book of spells and incantations, teaching sorcery both to appease and curse the demon world. The Atharva-Veda was based upon the "Aryan popular religion" of the time.

The initiation ceremony of TM is a ritual, the heart of which, is a Vedic hymn called the "Puja". The "Puja", a lengthy Mantra, is divided into three phases, and is recited in Sanskrit by the initiator or Adept, during the initiatory ritual, in order to produce an altered state of consciousness in the initiator and initiate. The initiate thus becomes passive and thereby receptive for the "Seed Mantra".[8]

The first phase of the "Puja", represents the "Apostolic succession" of the Shankara tradition of Hinduism, through which the "Holy Knowledge" of the TM Mantras passes. Each person mentioned is regarded and is exalted as a deity, worthy of worship.[9]

The second phase of the "Puja" is the actual offerings of fruit, flowers and white handkerchief brought by the initiate. The initiator or Adept places these before a picture of the Maharishi's dead master who is now presumably a god. The flowers are representative of life, the fruit is the seed of life, and the white handkerchief is symbolic of the cleansing of the spirit. 17 different items are offered in turn, while the initiator recites in Sanskrit a repeated verbal formula, which concludes each time with the words "I BOW DOWN".[10]

The third phase of the "Puja" is literally a hymn of praise and adoration to the departed Guru Dev. For example, the opening stanza consists of homage to the Hindu Holy Trinity, in the person of Guru Dev.[11]

At the end of the "Puja" the initiator or Adept bows down and invites the initiate to do likewise. The initiate participates both actively and passively in the initiatory ritual.[12]

After the "Puja" the initiate is given his Mantra which he repeats silently, until a pleasant sensation occurs.[13] The Maharishi has stated that this hypnotic recitation produces "such a state of mind . . . that is as if he (the initiate) has been deeply hypnotized."

The resultant of TM is behavior modification. Prominent individuals, including the Maharishi himself, have pointed out the very real similarities between TM and other modification techniques. The most obvious sign of this modification is the seemingly detached and passive attitude of the meditator as regards his present religion. This *religious neutralism* is necessary for the desired future goal of a one world religion—that of the BEAST.

The "World Plan" of TM calls for one TM teacher for every one thousand inhabitants of the earth.

The corporate umbrella for the American TM movement is the tax-exempt "World Plan Executive Council—U.S.", formerly called the "International Meditation Society" (IMS). Other groups are: "International Transcendental Movement", headquartered in Switzerland;

"Academy of Meditation" in Rishikesh, India; "Student International Meditation Society" (SIMS); "Maharishi International University" (MIU), formerly Parsons College of Iowa; "Maharishi European Research University" (MERU), located in Weggis, Switzerland; and KSCI-TV of Los Angeles. (The word MERU in Hindu mythology is a mountain in the center of the earth, the Abode of the Hindu deities.)[14]

Funding for the training of TM teachers has come from: The National Institute of Mental Health (NIMH); the VA; the National Science Foundation; NASA; the Civil Service Commission; the Bureau of Prisons; all three branches of the Armed Forces; and, of course, the Health, Education and Welfare Department (HEW).

This fact sheet on TM, unless otherwise noted, is based upon Chapter XII of "Brotherhood of Darkness," by Rex Myles.

1. National Educator, November, 1975
2. Ibid.
3. Los Angeles Times, May 12, 1974
4. TM: Penetrating the Veil of Deception; pamphlet published by the Spiritual Counterfeits Project, Berkeley, California
5. National Educator, November, 1975
6. Aquarian Pathfinder, (Yes, Inc.!), p. 101
7. Meditations of Maharishi Mahesh Yogi, P 17
8. TM: Penetrating the Veil of Deception
9. An English translation of Transcendental Meditation's initiatory Puja; pamphlet published by the Spiritual Counterfeits Project, Berkeley, California
10. Ibid.
11. Ibid.
12. Ibid.
13. TM: Penetrating the Veil of Deception
14. H. F. Wedeck and Wade Baskin, Dictionary of Spiritualism, (New York City, Philosophical Library, 1971), P 232

APPENDIX 10

Generally, before a child is given sex education, a permission slip is sent home for the parent to sign. We would like to share with you a letter sent by an Ohio mother to her child's teacher before permission was given.

Teacher's name:

Before I give permission for _____ to attend your sex education class, I would appreciate some questions answered.

1. Could I see all materials to be used in this class?
2. What are the titles of the films you will be using and what organization made or produced the films?
3. If you plan speakers from Planned Parenthood, I want to see the text of the speech or presentation before scheduled. Is this possible?
4. Will you emphasize the emotional and physical problems that are a major aspect of teenage sexual activity?
5. How are you going to present abortion?
6. Do you present VD as a serious problem or just a casual one?
7. What personal attitudes do you project about sex when teaching this class?
8. What changes in attitude do you expect from your students after presenting your material?
9. Do you plan to discuss alternate life-styles? How will you handle the homosexual life-style if it is brought up in class?

I trust _____ will not undergo harassment because he/she has a concerned mother. I also do not want the values and morals I taught my child, with respect to sex, to be undermined by the prevalent attitude that teenage sexual activity is permissible with the use of contraception.

Sincerely

Excerpted from a newsletter from Committee for Positive Education, 868 Kenmore, N.E., Warren, Ohio 44483. Used by permission.

CHRISTIAN HERALD ASSOCIATION AND ITS MINISTRIES

CHRISTIAN HERALD ASSOCIATION, founded in 1878, publishes The Christian Herald Magazine, one of the leading interdenominational religious monthlies in America. Through its wide circulation, it brings inspiring articles and the latest news of religious developments to many families. From the magazine's pages came the initiative for CHRISTIAN HERALD CHILDREN'S HOME and THE BOWERY MISSION, two individually supported not-for-profit corporations.

CHRISTIAN HERALD CHILDREN'S HOME, established in 1894, is the name for a unique and dynamic ministry to disadvantaged children, offering hope and opportunities which would not otherwise be available for reasons of poverty and neglect. The goal is to develop each child's potential and to demonstrate Christian compassion and understanding to children in need.

Mont Lawn is a permanent camp located in Bushkill, Pennsylvania. It is the focal point of a ministry which provides a healthful "vacation with a purpose" to children who without it would be confined to the streets of the city. Up to 1000 children between the ages of 7 and 11 come to Mont Lawn each year.

Christian Herald Children's Home maintains year-round contact with children by means of an *In-City Youth Ministry*. Central to its philosophy is the belief that only through sustained relationships and demonstrated concern can individual lives be truly enriched. Special emphasis is on individual guidance, spiritual and family counseling and tutoring. This follow-up ministry to inner-city children culminates for many in financial assistance toward higher education and career counseling.

THE BOWERY MISSION, located at 227 Bowery, New York City, has since 1879 been reaching out to the lost men on the Bowery, offering them what could be their last chance to rebuild their lives. Every man is fed, clothed and ministered to. Countless numbers have entered the 90-day residential rehabilitation program at the Bowery Mission. A concentrated ministry of counseling, medical care, nutrition therapy, Bible study and Gospel services awakens a man to spiritual renewal within himself.

These ministries are supported solely by the voluntary contributions of individuals and by legacies and bequests. Contributions are tax deductible. Checks should be made out either to CHRISTIAN HERALD CHILDREN'S HOME or to THE BOWERY MISSION.

Administrative Office: 40 Overlook Drive, Chappaqua, New York 10514
Telephone: (914) 769-9000